Research Software Engineering

Research Software Engineering: A Guide to the Open Source Ecosystem strives to give a big-picture overview and an understanding of the opportunities of programming as an approach to analytics and statistics. The book argues that a solid "programming" skill level is not only well within reach for many but also worth pursuing for researchers and business analysts. The ability to write a program leverages field-specific expertise and fosters interdisciplinary collaboration as source code continues to become an important communication channel. Given the pace of the development in data science, many senior researchers and mentors, alongside non-computer science curricula lack a basic software engineering component. This book fills the gap by providing a dedicated programming-with-data resource to both academic scholars and practitioners.

Key Features

- overview: breakdown of complex data science software stacks into core components
- applied: source code of figures, tables and examples available and reproducible solely with license cost-free, open source software
- reader guidance: different entry points and rich references to deepen the understanding of selected aspects

Matthias Bannert, Ph.D. gained his hands-on data science and data engineering at ETH Zürich in more than a decade of working for the KOF Swiss Economic Institute. Today, he works as a data engineering expert advisor at cynkra and supports ETH as a section lead in the innovation-minded KOF Lab. In 2021, he was a co-chair of useR!, the annual user conference of the R Project for Statistical Computing. He remains an active contributor to extension packages of the R language and the open source community in general.

CHAPMAN & HALL/CRC DATA SCIENCE SERIES

Reflecting the interdisciplinary nature of the field, this book series brings together researchers, practitioners, and instructors from statistics, computer science, machine learning, and analytics. The series will publish cutting-edge research, industry applications, and textbooks in data science.

The inclusion of concrete examples, applications, and methods is highly encouraged. The scope of the series includes titles in the areas of machine learning, pattern recognition, predictive analytics, business analytics, Big Data, visualization, programming, software, learning analytics, data wrangling, interactive graphics, and reproducible research.

Recently Published Titles

Practitioner's Guide to Data Science
Hui Lin and Ming Li

Natural Language Processing in the Real World
Text Processing, Analytics, and Classification
Jyotika Singh

Telling Stories with Data
With Applications in R
Rohan Alexander

Big Data Analytics
A Guide to Data Science Practitioners Making the Transition to Big Data
Ulrich Matter

Data Science for Sensory and Consumer Scientists
Thierry Worch, Julien Delarue, Vanessa Rios De Souza and John Ennis

Data Science in Practice
Tom Alby

Introduction to NFL Analytics with R
Bradley J. Congelio

Soccer Analytics: An Introduction Using R
Clive Beggs

Spatial Statistics for Data Science: Theory and Practice with R
Paula Moraga

Research Software Engineering: Research Software Engineering
Matthias Bannert

For more information about this series, please visit: https://www.routledge.com/
Chapman--HallCRC-Data-Science-Series/book-series/CHDSS

Research Software Engineering

A Guide to the Open Source Ecosystem

Matthias Bannert

CRC Press
Taylor & Francis Group
Boca Raton London New York

CRC Press is an imprint of the
Taylor & Francis Group, an **informa** business

A CHAPMAN & HALL BOOK

Designed cover image: © Matthias Bannert

First edition published 2024
by CRC Press
2385 NW Executive Center Drive, Suite 320, Boca Raton FL 33431

and by CRC Press
4 Park Square, Milton Park, Abingdon, Oxon, OX14 4RN

CRC Press is an imprint of Taylor & Francis Group, LLC

© 2024 Matthias Bannert

ISBN: 978-1-032-26164-5 (hbk)
ISBN: 978-1-032-26127-0 (pbk)
ISBN: 978-1-003-28689-9 (ebk)

DOI: 10.1201/978-1-003-28689-9

Typeset in Latin Modern font
by KnowledgeWorks Global Ltd.

Publisher's note: This book has been prepared from camera-ready copy provided by the authors.

Contents

List of Figures

List of Tables

Preface

> One of the things that Baidu did well early on was to create an internal platform for deep learning. What that did was enable engineers all across the company, including people who were not AI researchers, to leverage deep learning in all sorts of creative ways - applications that an AI researcher like me never would have thought of. – Andrew Ng

The vast majority of data has been created within the last decade. In turn, many fields of research are confronted with an unprecedented wealth of data. The sheer amount of information and the complexity of modern datasets continue to point a kind of researcher to programming approaches that had not considered programming to process data so far. *Research Software Engineering* aims at two things: First, to give a big picture overview and starting point to reach what the open source software community calls a "software carpentry" level. Second, to give an understanding of the opportunities of automation and reproducibility, as well as the effort to maintain the required environment. This book argues a solid programming skill level and self-operation is totally in reach for most researchers. And most importantly, investing is worth the effort: being able to code leverages field-specific expertise and fosters interdisciplinary collaboration as source code continues to become an important communication channel.

Figure 1: "Hackers wear hoodies, you know," mumbles Dr. Egghead as he pulls up his coat's hood and starts to figure out how his assistant got a week's work done in hours. (Source: own illustration.)

Acknowledgments

I am thankful for the inspiration, help and perspectives of everyone who contributed to this book at its different stages. There are several people and organizations that I would like to thank in particular.

First, thank you to David Grubbs at CRC Press for getting me started. From our first meeting at useR! in Toulouse, France, David helped streamline writing a book, and he kept adding value throughout the process with his remarks and contacts. I would like to thank Achim Zeileis who also played an important role at the early stage of my book project. Achim inspired me to become a co-host for useR! which led to many experiences that became important to this book. Our discussions about teaching amplified my motivation to have good material to accompany my own course – which eventually turned out to be one of the most important drivers.

In that regard, I would like to thank all participants of my *Hacking for ...* courses. Your insights, questions, feedback and semester projects have been invaluable to this project. Your field-specific expertise is inspirational not only to me, but also to readers of the book as it shows the broad relevance of the approach. I would like to thank ETH Zurich, in particularly the Department of Management, Technology and Economics (D-MTEC) and the KOF Swiss Economic Institute for hosting my ideas over the last 13 years. Thank you to educational developers Karin Brown and Erik Jentges; having teaching professionals with open ears and minds around helped to channel motivation and ideas into a course concept that continues to be popular among participants across departments and disciplines. Torbjørn Netland deserves credit for enabling this widespread interest. His early advice turned what was initially thought of as *Hacking for Economists* into *Hacking for Social Sciences*, which eventually became *Hacking for Science*.

Though this book is not exactly about the R programming language, I would like to thank the R community in particular because of its instrumental role in growing my own engagement and horizon of the open source ecosystem. My thanks go to statisticians Siegfried Heiler and Toni Stocker who pointed me to the R language almost 20 years ago. One of my most important learnings about how to leverage open source work may have come only 20 years later: In 2021, the community overcame the hurdles of the global COVID-19 pandemic that was unprecedented, at least in my lifetime, and held a virtual useR! conference that enabled a much larger and much more diverse group of participants to join (Joo et al. 2022).

Working with Rocío Joo, Dorothea Hug Peter, Heather Turner and Yanina Bellini Saibene has shown me the inclusion extra mile is not only worth the effort, but an inevitable mindset to bring our work as developers and scientists to the next level. Thank you, ladies! Thanks also to the local R user group in Zurich, Switzerland, who continues to show the practical relevance of open source through events. I want to mention the great people at my new employer, cynkra, too. Your influence on the community and therefore this book cannot be forgotten. Thank you for your support and open ears!

Last but not least, I would like to thank Emily Riederer for her time and patience discussing my thoughts and reviewing my drafts. Particulary, her ideas to streamline and balance my ideas at a stage where they were rather messy added great value. Admittedly, your constructive feedback has caused some extra work, but was instrumental to making this book useful and accessible to a wider audience – Thank you.

1

Introduction

Simply put, *Research Software Engineering* is the art of making our work deployable and functional on other machines.

1.1 Why Work Like a Software Engineer?

Why should a researcher or business analyst work Like a Software Engineer? First, because everybody and their grandmothers seem to work like software engineers. Statistical computing continues to be on the rise in many branches of research. Figure 1.1 shows the obvious trend in the sum of total R package downloads per month since 2015.

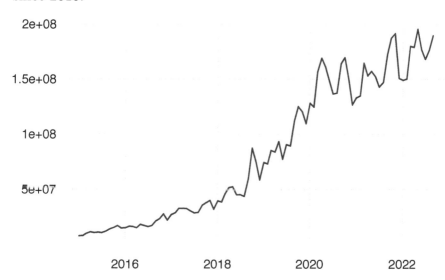

Figure 1.1: Monthly R Package Downloads. (Source: RStudio CRAN mirror.)

```
library(cranlogs)
library(dplyr)
library(lubridate)
library(tsbox)
top <- cranlogs::cran_top_downloads()

packs <- cranlogs::cran_downloads(
                              from = "2015-01-01",
                              to = "2022-09-30")

packs |>
  group_by(floor_date(date, "month")) |>
  summarize(m = sum(count)) |>
  ts_plot()
```

Bandwagonism aside, source code can be a tremendously sharp, unambiguous and international communication channel. Your web scraper does not work? Instead of reaching out in a clumsy but wordy cry for help, posting what you tried so far described by source code will often get you good answers within hours. Platforms like stackoverflow[1] or Crossvalidated[2] do not only store millions of questions and answers, they also gather a huge and active community to discuss issues. Plus, recent developments show that source code is not only useful to communicate with human experts. Have you tried to turn an idea into code or improve a piece of code by playing ping pong with chatGPT or Bing? Or think of feature requests: After a little code ping pong with the package author, your wish eventually becomes clearer. Let alone chats with colleagues and co-authors. Sharing code just works. Academic journals have found that out, too. Many outlets require you to make the data and source code behind your work available. Social Science Data Editors (Vilhuber et al. 2022) is a bleeding-edge project at the time of writing this, but it is already referred to by top-notch journals like *American Economic Review (AER)*.

---

[1]https://stackoverflow.com
[2]https://crossvalidated.com

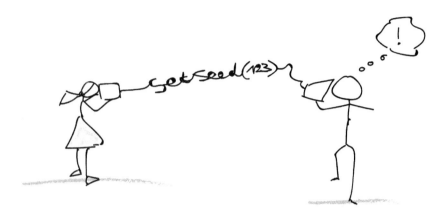

Figure 1.2: Source code is an unambiguous, interactive and global communication channel. (Source: own illustration.)

In addition to the above reproducibility and ability to share, code scales and automates. automation is very convenient; like when you want to download data, process and create the same visualization and put it on your website any given Sunday. automation is inevitable; like when you have to gather daily updates from different outlets or work through thousands of .pdfs.

Last but not least, programming enables you to do many things you couldn't do without being an absolute guru (if at all) if it wasn't for programming. Take visualization, for example. Go check the D3 Examples at https://d3js.org/. Now, try to do that in Excel. If you did these things in Excel, it would make you an absolute spreadsheet visualization Jedi, probably missing out on other time-consuming skills to master. Yet, with decent, carpentry-level programming skills you can already do so many spectacular things while not really specializing and staying very flexible.

1.2   Why Work Like an Operations Engineer?

While software *development* has become closer to many researchers, *operations*, the second part of the term *DevOps*, is much further away from the average researcher or business analyst. Why even think about operations? Because we can afford to do so. Operations have become so much more accessible in recent years, that many applications can be dealt with single-handedly. Though one's production applications may still be administered by operations professionals, the ability to create and run a proof of concept from scratch is an invaluable skill. A running example says more than a 15-page specification that fails to translate business talk into tech talk. The other way around, something to look at an early stage helps to acquire funds and convince managers and other collaborators.

But people without a computer engineering background are by no means limited to proof of concepts these days. Trends like cloud computing and software-as-a-service products help developers focus on their expertise and limit the amount of knowledge needed to host a service in secure and highly available fashion.

Also, automation is key to the DevOps approach and an important reason why DevOps thinking is also very well suited for academic researchers and business analysts. So-called *continuous integration* can help to enforce a battery of quality checks such as unit tests or installation checks. Let's say a push to a certain branch of a git repository leads to the checks and tests. In a typical workflow, successful completion of quality checks triggers continuous deployment to a blog, rendering into a paper or interactive data visualization.

By embracing both parts of the *DevOps* approach, researchers do not only gain extra efficiency, but more importantly they improve reproducibility and therefore accountability and quality of their work. The effect of a DevOps approach on quality control is not limited to reproducible research in a publication sense only, but also enforces rules during collaboration: no matter who contributes, the contribution gets gut-checked and only deployed if checks passed. Similar to the well established term *software carpentry* that advocates a solid, application minded understanding of programming with data, I suggest a carpentry-level understanding of development and operations is desirable for the programming data analyst.

1.3   How To Read This Book?

The focal goal of this book is to map out the open source ecosystem, identify neuralgic components and give you an idea of how to improve not only in programming but also in navigating the wonderful but vast open source world. Chapter 2 is the road map for this book: it describes and classifies the different parts of the open source stack and explains how these pieces relate to each other. Subsequent chapters highlight core elements of the open source toolbox one at a time and walk through applied examples, mostly written in the R language.

This book is the companion I wish I had when I started an empirical, data intensive PhD in economics. Yet, the book is written years after my PhD was completed and with the hindsight of more than 10 years in academia. *Research Software Engineering* is written based on the experience of helping students and seasoned researchers of different fields with their data management, processing and communication of results.

If you are confident in your ambition to amp up your programming to at least solid software carpentry level[3] within the next few months, I suggest getting an idea of your starting point relative to this book. The upcoming *backlog* section is essentially a list of suggested to-dos on your way to solid software carpentry. Obviously, you may have cleared a few tasks of this backlog before reading this book which is fine. On the other hand, you might not know about some of the things that are listed in the *requirement* section,

---

[3]https://software-carpentry.org/

which is fine, too. The backlog and requirements section just mean to give you some orientation.

If you do not feel committed, revisit the previous section, discuss the need for programming with peers from your domain and possibly talk to a seasoned R or Python programmer. Motivation and commitment are key to the endurance needed to develop programming into a skill that truly leverages your domain-specific expertise.

1.4   Backlog

If you can confidently say you can check all or most of the below, you have reached *carpentry* level in developing and running your applications. Even if this level is your starting point, you might find a few useful tips or simply may come to cherry-pick. In case you are rather unfamiliar with most of the below, the contextualization, the classification and overview of tools is likely the most valuable help this book provides.

A solid, applied understanding of **git version control** and the **collaboration workflow associated with git** does not only help you stay ahead of your own code; git proficiency makes you a team player. If you are not familiar with commits, pulls, pushes, branches, forks and pull requests, *Research Software Engineering* will open up a new world for you. An introduction to industry standard collaboration makes you fit into a plethora of (software) teams around the globe – in academia and beyond.

Your backlog en route to a researcher who is comfortable in *Research Software Engineering* obviously contains a **strategy to improve your programming** itself. To work with data in the long run, an idea of the **challenges of data management** from persistent storage to access restrictions should complement your programming. Plus, modern data-driven science often has to handle datasets so large, which is when **infrastructure** other than local desktops come into play. Yet, high performance computing (HPC) is by far not the only reason it is handy for a researcher to have a basic understanding of **infrastructure**. **Communication** of results, including data dissemination or interactive online reports require the content to be served from a server with permanent online access. Basic workflow **automation** of regular procedures, e.g., for a repeated extract-transform-load (ETL) process to update data, is a low-hanging (and very useful) fruit for a programming researcher.

The case studies at the end of the book are not exactly a backlog item like the above but still a recommended read. The case studies in this book are hands-on programming examples – mostly written in R – to showcase tasks from application programming interface (API) usage to geospatial visualization in reproducible fashion. Reading and actually running other developers' code not only improve one's own code, but helps to see what makes code inclusive and what hampers comprehensibility.

1.5 Requirements

Even though *Research Software Engineering* aims to be inclusive and open to a broad audience with different starting points, several prerequisites exist to get the most out of this book. I recommend you have made your first experience with an interpreted programming language like R or Python. Be aware though that experience from a stats or math course does not automatically make you a programmer, as these courses are rightfully focused on their own domain. Books like *R for Data Science* (Hadley Wickham and Grolemund 2017) or websites like the *The Carpentries*[4] help to solidify your data science minded, applied programming. *Advanced R* (Hadley Wickham 2019), despite its daunting title, is an excellent read to get past the superficial kind of understanding of R that we might acquire from a first encounter in a stats course.

---

[4]https://carpentries.org/

A certain familiarity with *console/terminal basics* will help the reader sail smoothly. At the end of the day, there are no real must-have requirements to benefit from this book. The ability to self-reflect on one's starting point remains the most important requirement to leverage the book.

Research Software Engineering willingly accepts to be overwhelming at times. Given the variety of topics touched on in an effort to show the big picture, I encourage the reader to remain relaxed about a few blanks even when it comes to fundamentals. The open source community offers plenty of great resources to selectively upgrade skills. This book intends to show how to evaluate the need for help and how to find the right sources. If none of the above means something to you, though, I recommend making yourself comfortable with the basics of some of the above fields before you start to read this book.

2

Stack: A Developer's Toolkit

The goal of this chapter (and probably the most important goal of this entire book) is to help you see the big picture of which tool does what. The following sections will group common programming-with-data components by purpose. All of the resulting groups represent aspects of programming with data, and I will move on to discuss these groups in a dedicated chapter each.

Figure 2.1: Aaaaaaah! Don't panic, Dr. Egghead! All these components are here to help you and you won't need all of them from the start. (Source: own illustration.)

Just like natural craftsmen, digital carpenters depend on their toolbox and their mastery of it. A project's *stack* is what developers

Table 2.1: Components of Data Science Stack

Component	Choice
Interpreter/Language	R, Python, JavaScript
IDE/Editor	R Studio, VS Code, Sublime
Version Control	Git
Project Management	GitHub, GitLab
database	PostgreSQL
"Virtual" Environments	Docker
Communication (Visualization, Web)	Node, Quasar (vue.js)
Website Hosting	Netlify, GitHub Pages
Workflow automation	Apache Airflow
Continous Integration	Woodpecker, GitLab CI, GitHub Actions

call the choice of tools used in a project. Even though different flavors come down to personal preferences, there is a lot of common ground in *programming with data* stacks. Table 2.1 shows some of the components I use most often grouped by their role. Of course, this is a personal choice. Obviously, I do not use *all* of these components in every single small project. *Git, R* and *R Studio* would be a good minimal version.

Throughout this book, often a choice for one piece of software needs to be made to illustrate things. To get the most out of the book, keep in mind that these choices are examples and try to focus on the role of an item in the big picture.

2.1   Programming Language

In Statistical Computing, the interface between the researcher and the computation node is almost always an interpreted programming language as opposed to a compiled one. Compiled languages like

C++ require the developer to write source code and compile, i.e., translate source code into what a machine can work with *before* runtime. The result of the compilation process is a binary which is specific to an operating system. Hence, you will need one version for Windows, one for OSX and one for Linux if you intend to reach a truly broad audience with your program. The main advantage of a compiled language is speed in terms of computing performance, because the translation into machine language does not happen during runtime. A reduction of development speed and increase in required developer skills are the downside of using compiled languages.

> Big data is like teenage sex: everyone talks about it, nobody really knows how to do it, everyone thinks everyone else is doing it, so everyone claims they are doing it. – Dan Ariely, Professor of Psychology and Behavioral Economics on X[1]

The above quote became famous in the hacking data community, not only because of the provocative, fun part of it, but also because of the implicit advice behind it. Given the enormous gain in computing power in recent decades, and also methodological advances, interpreted languages are often fast enough for many social science problems. And even if it turns out, your data grow out of your setup, a well-written proof of concept written in an interpreted language can be a formidable blueprint. **Source code is turning into an important scientific communication channel.** Put your money on it, your interdisciplinary collaborator from the High Performance Computing (HPC) group will prefer some Python code as a briefing for their C++ or Fortran program over a wordy description out of your field's ivory tower.

Interpreted languages are a bit like pocket calculators, you can look at intermediate results, line-by-line. R and Python are the most popular open source software (OSS) choices for hacking with data, Julia (Bezanson et al. 2017) is an up-and-coming, performance-focused language with a much slimmer ecosystem. A bit of JavaScript can't

---

[1]https://x.com/danariely/status/287952257926971392

hurt for advanced customization of graphics and online communication of your results.

2.2　Interaction Environment

While the fact that a software developer needs to choose a programming language to work with is rather obvious, the need to compose and customize an environment to interact with the computer is much less obvious to many. Understandably so because, outside of programming, software such as word processors, video or image editors presents itself to the user as a single program. That single program takes the user's input, processes the input (in memory) and stores a result on disk for persistence – often in a proprietary, program specific format.

Yet, despite all the understanding for nonchalantly saying we keep documents **in** Word or data **in** R Studio, it's beyond nerdy nit-picking when I insist that data are kept in files (or databases) – **not** in a program. And that R is **not** R Studio: This sloppy terminology contributes to making us implicitly accept that our office documents live in one single program. (And that there is only one way to find and edit these files: through said program).

It is important to understand that source code of essentially any programming languages is a just a plain text file and therefore can be edited in any editor. Editors come in all shades of gray: from lean, minimal code highlighting support to full-fledged integrated development environments (IDEs) with everything from version control integration to sophisticated debugging.

Which way of interaction the developer likes better is partly a matter of personal taste, but it also depends on the programming language, the team's form of collaboration and size of the project. In addition to a customized editor, most developers use some form of a console to communicate with their operating system. The ability to send commands instead of clicking is not only reproducible and shareable, but it also outpaces mouse movement by a lot when commands come in batches. Admittedly, configuration, practice and getting up to speed takes time, but once you have properly customized the way you interact with your computer when writing code, you will never look back.

In any case, make sure to customize your development environment: choose the themes you like, make sure the cockpit you spent your day in is configured properly and feels comfy.

2.3   Version Control

To buy into the importance of managing one's code professionally may be the single most important take-away from this book. Being able to work with will help you fit into numerous different teams that have contact points with data science and programming, let alone if you become part of a programming or data science team.

While has a long history dating back to CVS[2] and SVN[3], the good news for the learner is, that there is a single dominant approach when it comes to in the data analysis world. Despite the fact that its predecessors and alternatives such as Mercurial are still around, git[4] is the one you have to learn. To learn more about the history of and approaches other than git, Eric Sink's *Version Control by Example* (Sink 2011) is for you.

So what does git do for us as researchers? How is it different from Dropbox?

```
git does not work like dropbox. git is not like dropbox.
git does not work like dropbox. git is not like dropbox.
git does not work like dropbox. git is not like dropbox.
git does not work like dropbox. git is not like dropbox.
```

---

[2]Concurrent Versions System: https://cvs.nongnu.org/
[3]Apache Subversion
[4]https://git-scm.com/book/en/v2/Getting-Started-About-Version-Control

```
git does not work like dropbox. git is not like dropbox.
git does not work like dropbox. git is not like dropbox.
```

The idea of thinking of a sync is what interferes with comprehension of the benefit of (which is why I hate that git GUIs call it "sync" anyway to avoid irritation of user's initial beliefs.). Git is a decentralized system that keeps track of a history of semantic commits. Those commits may consist of changes to multiple files. A commit message summarizes the gist of a contribution. *Diffs* allow comparing different versions.

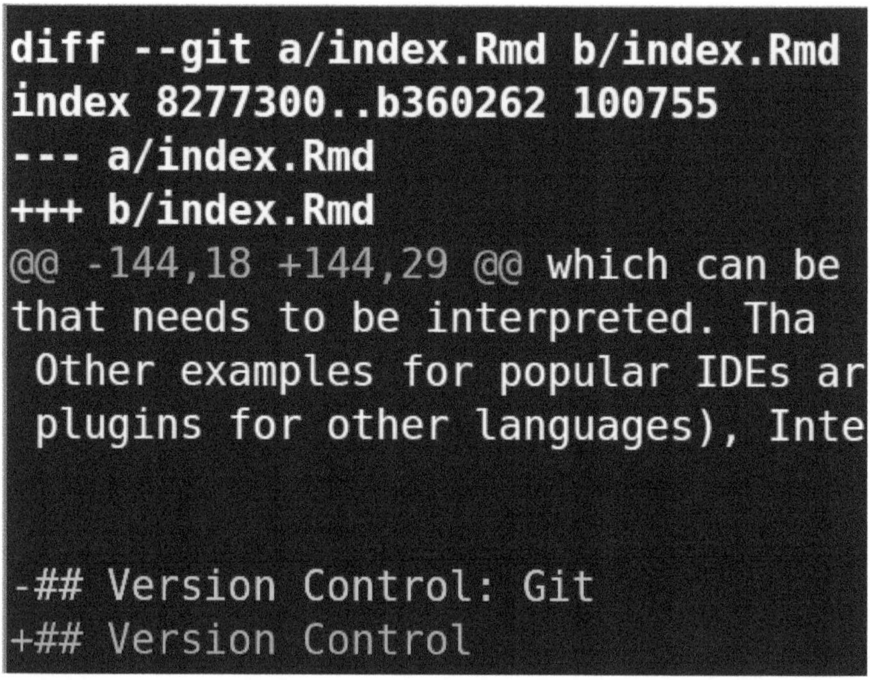

```
diff --git a/index.Rmd b/index.Rmd
index 8277300..b360262 100755
--- a/index.Rmd
+++ b/index.Rmd
@@ -144,18 +144,29 @@ which can be
that needs to be interpreted. Tha
 Other examples for popular IDEs ar
 plugins for other languages), Inte


-## Version Control: Git
+## Version Control
```

Figure 2.2: The *diff* output shows an edit during the writing of this book. The line preceded by '-' was replaced with the line preceded by '+'.

Git is well suited for any kind of text file, whether it is source code from Python or C++, or some text written in Markdown or LaTeX. Binaries like .pdfs or Word documents are possible, too, but certainly not the type of file for which git is really useful. This book contains a detailed, applied introduction tailored to researchers in a dedicated chapter, so let's dwell with the above contextualization for a bit.

2.4 Data Management

One implication of bigger datasets and/or bigger teams is the need to manage data. Particularly when projects establish themselves or update their data regularly, well-defined processes, consistent storage and possibly access management become relevant. But even if you worked alone, it can be very helpful to have an idea about data storage in files systems, memory consumption and archiving data for good.

Data come in various forms and dimensions, potentially deeply nested. Yet, researchers and analysts are mostly trained to work with one-row-one-observation formats, in which columns typically represent different variables. In other words, two-dimensional representation of data remains the most common and intuitive form of data to many. Hence, office software offers different, text-based and proprietary spreadsheet file formats. On disk, comma separated files (.csv)[5] are probably the purest representation of two-dimensional data that can be processed comfortably by any programming language and that can be read by many programs. Other formats such as .xml or .json allow storing even deeply nested data.

In-memory, that is when working interactively with programming languages such as R or Python, data.frames are the most common representation of two-dimensional data. Data.frames, their progressive relatives like tibbles or data.tables and the ability to manipulate them in reproducible, shareable and discussible fashion is the first superpower upgrade over pushing spreadsheets. Plus, other representation such as arrays, dictionaries or lists represent nested data in memory. Though in-memory data manipulation is very appealing, memory is limited and needs to be managed.

---

[5]Some dialects use different separators like ';' or tabs, partly because of regional differences like the use of commas as decimal delimiters.

Making the most of the memory available is one of the driving forces behind extensions of the original data.frame concept.

The other obvious limitation of data in memory is the lack of persistent storage. Therefore, in-memory data processing needs to be combined with file based storage are a database. The good news is that languages like R and Python are well-equipped to interface with a plethora of file-based approaches as well as databases. So well, that I often recommend these languages to researchers who work with other less-equipped tools, solely as an intermediate layer.

To evaluate which relational (essentially SQL) or non-relational database to pick up just seems like the next daunting task of stack choice. Luckily, in research, first encounters with a database are usually passive, in the sense that you want to query data from a source. In other words, the choice has been made for you. So unless you want to start your own data collection from scratch, simply sit back, relax and let the internet battle out another conceptual war. For now, let's just be aware of the fact that a data management game plan should be part of any analysis project.

2.5   Infrastructure

For researchers and business analysts who want to program with data, the starting infrastructure is very likely their own desktop or notebook computer. Nowadays, this already means access to remarkable computing power suited for many tasks.

Yet, it is good to be aware of the many reasons that can turn the infrastructure choice from a no-brainer into a question with many options and consequences. Computing power, repeated or scheduled tasks, hard-to-configure or non-compatible runtime environment, online publication or high availability may be some of the needs that make you think about infrastructure beyond your own notebook.

Today, thanks to software-as-a-service (SaaS) offers and cloud computing, none of the above needs imply running a server, let alone a computing center on your own. Computing has not only become more powerful over the last decade, but also more accessible. Entry hurdles are lower than ever. Many needs are covered by services that do not require serious upfront investment. It has become convenient to try and let the infrastructure grow with the project.

From a researcher's and analyst's perspective, one of the most noteworthy infrastructure developments of recentness may be the arrival of *containers* in data analysis. Containers are isolated, single-purpose environments that run either on a single container host or with an orchestrator in a cluster. Although technically different from virtual machines, we can regard containers as virtual computers running on a computer for now. With containers, data analysts can create isolated, single purpose environments that allow to reproduce analysis even after one's system was upgraded and with it all the libraries used to run the analysis. Or think of some exotic LaTeX configuration, Python environment or database drivers that you just can't manage to run on your local machine. Bet there is a container blueprint (aka image) around online for exactly this purpose.

> Premature optimization is the root of all evil. – Donald Knuth.

On the flip side, product offerings and therefore our options have become a fast-growing, evolving digital jungle. So, rather than trying to keep track (and eventually loosing it) of the very latest gadgets, this book intends to show a big picture{big picture} overview and pass on a strategy to evaluate the need to add to your infrastructure. Computing power, availability, specific services and collaboration are the main drivers for researchers to look beyond their own hardware. Plus, public exposure, i.e., running a website as discussed in the publishing section, asks for a web host beyond our local notebooks.

2.6   Automation

"Make repetitive work fun again!" could be the claim of this section. Yet, it's not just the typical intern's or student assistant's job that we would love to automate. Regular ingestion of data from an application programming interface (API) or a web scraping process are one form of reoccurring tasks, often called cron jobs after the Linux cron command, which is used to schedule execution of Linux commands. Regular computation of an index, triggered by incoming data would be a less time-focused, but more event-triggered example of an automated task.

The one trending form of automation, though, is *continuous integration/continuous development (CI/CD)*. *CI/CD* processes are typically closely linked to a git repository and are triggered by a particular action done to the repository. For example, in case some pre-defined part (branch) of a git repository gets updated, an event is triggered and some process starts to run on some machine (usually some container). Builds of software packages are very common use cases of such a *CI/CD* process. Imagine you are developing an R package and want to run all the tests you've written, create the documentation and test whether the package can be installed. Once you've made your changes and push to your remote git repository, your push triggers the tests, the check, the documentation rendering and the installation. Potentially a push to the main branch of your repository could even deploy a package that cleared all of the above to your production server.

Rendering documentation, e.g., from Markdown to HTML into a website or presentation or a book like this one is a very similar example of a CI/CD process. Major git providers like Gitlab (GitLab CI/CD) or GiTHub (GitHub Actions) offer CI/CD tool integration. In addition, standalone services like CircleCI can be used as well as open source, self-hosted software like Woodpecker CI[6].

---

[6]https://woodpecker-ci.org/

2.7 Communication Tools

Its community is one of the reasons for the rise of open source software over the last decades. Particularly, newcomers would miss a great chance for a kick-start into programming if they did not connect with the community. Admittedly, not all the community's communication habits are for everyone, yet it is important to make your choices and pick up a few channels.

Chat clients like Slack, Discord or the Internet Relay Chat (IRC) (for the pre-millenials among readers) are the most direct form of asynchronous communication. Though many of the modern alternatives are not open source themselves, they offer free options and remain popular in the community despite self-hosted approaches such as matrix[7] along with Element[8]. Many international groups around data science and statistical computing such as RLadies or the Society of Research Software Engineering have Slack spaces that are busy 24/7 around the world.

Social media is less directed and more easily consumed in a passive fashion than a chat space. Over the last decade, *X*, formerly known as twitter, has been a very active and reliable resource for good reads but has seen parts of the community switch to more independent platforms such as Mastodon[9]. Linkedin is another suitable option to connect and find input, particularly in parts of the world where other platforms are less popular. Due to its activity, social media is also a great way to stay up-to-date with the latest developments.

Mailing lists are another, more old-fashioned form to discuss things. They do not require a special client and just an e-mail address to subscribe to their regular updates. If you intend to avoid social media, as well as signing up at knowledge sharing platforms such

---

[7]https://matrix.org/
[8]https://element.io/
[9]https://mastodon.social/

as stackoverflow.com[10] or reddit[11], mailing lists are a good way to get help from experienced developers.

Issue trackers are one form of communication that is often under-estimated by newcomers. Remotely hosted git repositories, e.g., repositories hosted at GitHub or GitLab, typically come with an integrated issue trackers to report bugs. The community discusses a lot more than problems on issue trackers: feature requests are a common use case, and even the future direction of an open source project may be affected substantially by discussions in its issue tracker.

2.8   Publishing and Reporting

Data analysis hopefully yields results that the analyst intends to report internally within their organization or share with the broader public. This has led to a plethora of options on the reporting end. Actually, data visualization and reproducible, automated report-ing are two of the main drivers researchers and analysts turn to programming for their data analysis.

In general, we can distinguish between two forms of output: pdf-like, print-oriented output and HTML-centered web content. Recent tool chains have enabled analysts without strong backgrounds in web frontend development (HTML/CSS/JavaScript) to create nifty reports and impressive, interactive visualizations. Frameworks like R Shiny or Python Dash even allow creating complex interactive websites.

Notebooks that came out of the Python world established them-selves in many other languages implementing the idea of combining text with code chunks that get executed when the text is rendered to HTML or PDF. This allows researchers to describe, annotate and discuss results while sharing the code that produced the results

---

[10]https://stackoverflow.com
[11]https://reddit.com

described. In academia, progressive scholars and journals embrace this form of creating manuscripts as *reproducible research* that improves trust in the presented findings.

Besides academic journals that started to require researchers to hand in their results in reproducible fashion, reporting based on so-called static website generators[12] has taken data blogs and reporting outlets including presentations by storm. Platforms like GitHub render Markdown files to HTML automatically, displaying formatted plain text as a decent website. Services such as Netlify allow using a broad variety of build tools to render input that contains text and code.

Centered around web browsers to display the output, HTML reporting allows creating simple reports, blogs, entire books (like this one) or presentation slides for talks. But thanks to document converters like Pandoc and a typesetting juggernaut called LaTeX, rendering sophisticated .pdf is possible, too. Some environments even allow rendering to proprietary word processor formats.

---

[12]As opposed to content management systems (CMS) that keep content in a database and put content and layout template together when users visit a website, static website generators render a website once triggered by an event. If users want to update a static website, they simply rerun the render process and push the HTML output of said process online.

3

Programming 101

Obviously, the craft of *programming* is essential to handling data with a programming language. Though programming languages can differ quite a bit from each other, there is common ground and an approach to programming that is crucial to understand and important to learn by – particularly for programmers without a formal computer science background. This chapter points researchers, analysts and data scientists to the low-hanging, high-impact fruits of software engineering.

Programming is a form of communication, a form of communication with others and also with your future self. It actually may be the best way to define complex contexts in reproducible fashion. Therefore, source code needs to be written in inclusive fashion. Programming needs to be seen as a chance to make complexity accessible to those who are not experts in a particular domain. The fact that programs actually run makes them more accessible to many than formal mathematical definitions.

The programming examples in this book mostly stick to the R language, which is easy to install and run on one's own local computer. All the concepts shown easily transfer to other languages. Though potentially a bit more tricky to install and run across operating systems, Python would have been an equally good choice. There had to be a decision for one language for this book.

3.1 The Choice That Doesn't Matter

The very first (and intimidating) choice a novice hacker faces is which is the programming language to learn. Unfortunately, the medium popularly summed up as the internet offers a lot of really, fantastic advice on the matter. The problem is, however, that this advice does not necessarily agree which language is the best for research. In the realm of data science – get accustomed to that label if you are a scientist who works with data – the debate basically comes down to two languages: The R Language for Statistical Computing and Python.

At least to me, there is only one valid advice: **It simply does not matter.** If you stick around in data science long enough, you will eventually get in touch with both languages and, in turn, learn both. There is a huge overlap of what you can do with either of those languages. R came out of the rather specific domain of statistics more than 25 years ago and made its way to a more general programming language thanks to over 20K extension packages (and counting). Built by a mathematician, Python continues to be as general purpose as it has ever been. But it got more scientific, thanks to extension packages of its own such as pandas[1], SciPy[2] or NumPy[3]. As a result, there is a huge overlap of what both languages can do, and both will extend your horizon in unprecedented fashion if you did not use a full-fledged programming language for your analysis beforehand.

But why is there such a heartfelt debate online if it doesn't matter? Let's pick up a random argument from this debate: R is easier to set up and Python is better for machine learning. If you worked with Java or another environment that's rather tricky to get going, you are hardened and might not cherish easy onboarding. If you got frustrated before you really started, you might feel otherwise.

---

[1]https://pandas.pydata.org/
[2]https://www.scipy.org/
[3]https://numpy.org/

Figure 3.1: R: "Dplyr smokes pandas." Python: "But Keras is better for ML!" Language wars can be entertaining, sometimes spectacular, but are essentially just useless. (Source: own illustration).

You may just have been unlucky making guesses about a not so well-documented paragraph, trying to reproduce a nifty machine learning blog post. Or imagine the frustration in case just had installed the wrong version of Python or did not manage to make sense of *virtualenv* right from the beginning.

The point is, rest assured, if you just start doing analytics using a programming language, both languages are guaranteed to carry you a long way. There is no way to tell for sure which one will be the more dominant language 10 years from now, or whether both will be around holding their ground the way they do now. But once you reached a decent software carpentry level in either language, it will help you a lot learning the other. If your peers work with R, start with R; if your close community works with Python, start with Python. If you are in for the longer run, either language will help you understand the concepts and ideas of programming with data. Trust me, there will be a natural opportunity to get to know the other.

If you associate programming more often than not with hours of fiddling, tweaking and fighting to galvanize approaches found online, this chapter is for you. Don't expect lots of syntax. If you came for examples of useful little programs from data visualization to parallel computing, check out the Case Studies.

The following sections share a blueprint to go from explorative script to production-ready package. Organize your code and accompany the evolution of your project: start out with experiments, define your interface, narrow down to a proof of concept and scale up. Hopefully, the tips, tricks and the guidance in this chapter will help you to experience the rewarding feeling of a software project coming together like a plan originated by Hannibal Smith[4].

3.2 Plan Your Program

How much planning ahead is optimal for your project ultimately depends on your experience, number of collaborators and the size of your project. But still, a rough standard checklist helps any project.

3.2.1 Think Library!

The approach that I find practical for applied, empirical research projects involving code is: think library. Think package. Think *reusable* code. Don't think you can't do it. Let me demystify packages for you: **Packages are nothing but source code organized in folders following some convention.** Thanks to modern IDEs, it has never been easier to stay inline with conventions. Editors like RStudio ship with built-in support to create package skeletons with a few clicks. Thousands of open source extension packages allow you to learn from their structure. Tutorials like

---

[4]Google me!

Packaging Python Projects[5] or Hadley Wickham's book *R Packages (H. Wickham 2015) explain how to create packages good enough to make the official PyPi or CRAN package repositories.

In other words, it is unlikely that someone with moderate experience comes with the best folder structure ever invented. Sure, every project is different and not every aspect (folder) is needed in every project. Nevertheless, there are well-established blueprints, guides and conventions that suit almost any project. Unlike Office type of projects which center around one single file, understand that a research project will live in a folder with many subfolders and files. Not in one single file.

Trust me on this one: The package approach will pay off early. Long before you ever thought about publishing your package. Write your own function definition, rather than just calling functions line-by-line. Write code as if you need to make sure it runs on another computer. Write code as if you need to maintain it.

Go from scripts like this

```
# This is just data for the sake of
# reproducible example
set.seed(123)
d1 <- rnorm(1000)
d2 <- rnorm(1000)


# let's create some custom descriptive
# stats summary for the data generated above
d1_mean <- mean(d1)
d1_sd <- sd(d1)
d1_q <- quantile(d1)
desc_stats_d1 <- list(d1_mean = d1_mean,
                      d1_sd = d1_sd,
                      d1_q = d1_q)


d2_mean <- mean(d2)
```

[5]https://packaging.python.org/tutorials/packaging-projects/

```
d2_sd <- sd(d2)
d2_q <- quantile(d2)
desc_stats_d2 <- list(d2_mean = d2_mean,
                      d2_sd = d2_sd,
                      d2_q = d2_q)
```

To function definitions and calls like that

```
# Imagine you had thousand of datasets.
# Imagine you wanted to add some other stats
# Imagine all the error prone c&p with
# the above solution.
# Think of how much easier this is to document.
# This is automation. Not cooking.
create_basic_desc <- function(distr){
  out <- list(
    mean = mean(distr),
    sd = sd(distr),
    quantiles = quantile(distr)
  )
  out
}
```

```
create_basic_desc(d1)
```

```
$mean
[1] 0.01612787

$sd
[1] 0.991695

$quantiles
          0%           25%           50%           75%          100%
-2.809774679 -0.628324243  0.009209639  0.664601867  3.241039935
```

```
create_basic_desc(d2)
```

```
$mean
[1] 0.04246525

$sd
[1] 1.009674

$quantiles
         0%         25%         50%         75%        100%
-3.04786089 -0.65322296  0.05485238  0.75345037  3.39037082
```

Start to document functions and their parameters using Roxygen (Hadley Wickham et al. 2022) syntax, and you're already very close to creating your first package.

> **Tip**
>
> Hit Cmd+Alt+Shift+R[a] while inside a function definition with your cursor. When working with R Studio, it will create a nifty Roxygen skeleton with all your function's parameters.
>
> ────────────────
> [a]On Windows/Linux use Ctrl instead of Cmd.

```
#' Create Basic Descriptive Statistics
#'
#' Creates means, standard deviations and default
#' quantiles from an numeric input vector.
#'
#' @param distr numeric vector drawn from an
#' arbitraty distribution.
#' @export
create_basic_desc <- function(distr){
  out <- list(
    mean = mean(distr),
    sd = sd(distr),
    quantiles = quantile(distr)
  )
  out
}
```

Writing *reusable code* will improve your ability to remember syntax and apply concepts to other problems. The more you do it, the easier and more natural it becomes. Just like a toddler figuring out how to speak in a natural language. At first, progress seems small, but once kids understand the bits and pieces of a language, they start building at a remarkable speed, learn and never forget again.

3.2.2 Documentation

First things first. Write the first bit of documentation before your first line of code. Documentation **written** with hindsight will always be written with an all-knowing, smartest-person-in-the-room mindset and the motivation of someone who already gave their best programming. Understand, I am not talking about the fine-tuning here, but about a written outline. Describe **how** parts of the code are going to do stuff. Also, examples can't hurt to illustrate what you meant. Research projects often take breaks, and getting back to work after months should be as easy as possible.

Pseudocode is a good way of writing up such an outline documentation. Take a simple application programming interface (API) wrapper, for example. Assume there is an API that returns numeric IDs of hit entries when queried for keywords. These IDs can be passed on to yet another endpoint, to obtain a profile. A rough game plan for an API Wrapper could look like this:

```
# function:
# keyword_search(
#   keyword,
#   url = "https://some.default.url.com"
#)
# returns numeric ids according to some
# api documentation

# function: query_profile(vec_in_ids)
# a json object that should be immediately
```

```
# turned into list by the function,
# returns list of properties
```

Documentation should use your ecosystem's favorite documentation framework. Yet, your comments within the code are the raw, initial form of documentation. Comments help to understand key parts of a program as well as caveats. Comments help tremendously during development time, when debugging or coming back to a project. Let alone when joining a project started by others.

While pseudocode where comments mimmick code itself is the exception to that rule, good comments should always follow the **not-what-but-why** principle. Usually, most high-level programming languages are fairly easy to read and remind of rudimentary English. Therefore, a *what* comment like this is considered rather useless:

```
# compute the cumulative sum of a vector
cumsum(c(T,F,F,F,F,T,F,F,T,F,F,F,T))
```

Whereas this *why* comment may actually be helpful:

```
# use the fact that TRUE is actually stored as 1
# to create a sequence until the next true
# this is useful for splitting the data later on.
cumsum(c(T,F,F,F,F,T,F,F,T,F,F,F,T))
```

Comment on why you do things, especially with which plan for future use in mind. Doing so will certainly foster exchange with others who enter or re-visit the code at a later stage (including yourself).

3.2.3   Design Your Interface

In many languages, it is fairly common to define the data type of both: the input and the output[6]. Though doing so is not necessary

---

[6]See statically typed language vs. dynamically typed language.

in R, it is good practice to define the types of all parameters and results in your comments/documentation.

Once you know a bit more about your direction of travel, it's time to think about how to modularize your program. How do different parts of the program play together? How do users interact with your program? Will your code just act as a storage pit of tools, a loose collection of commands for ad hoc use? Are others using the program, too? Will there be machine-to-machine interaction? Do you need a graphical user interface (GUI) like a Shiny app?

These questions will determine whether you use a strictly functional approach[7], a rudimentary form of object orientation like S3[8] (Hadley Wickham 2019), a stricter implementation like [R6 (Chang 2021) or something completely exotic. There are plenty of great resources out there, so I will not elaborate on this for the moment. The main message of this section is: Think about the main use case. Is it interactive? Is it a program that runs in batch, typically? Do your users code? Would they prefer a GUI?

3.2.4 Dependencies

One important word of advice for novice package developers is to think about your dependencies. Do not take dependencies lightly. Of course, it is intriguing to stand on the shoulders of giants. Isn't R great because of its over 20K extension packages? Isn't exactly this was made R such as popular language?

Yes, extension packages are cool. Yes, the ease with which CRAN packages are distributed is cool. But, just because packages are easy to install and free of license costs, it does not mean leaning on plenty of packages comes at no costs: One needs to stay informed about updates, issues, breaking changes or undesired interdependencies between packages.

The problem is mitigated a bit when (a) package is required in an interactive script and (b) one is working with a very popular

---

[7]http://adv-r.had.co.nz/Functional-programming.html
[8]http://adv-r.had.co.nz/OO-essentials.html

package. Well-managed packages with a lot of reverse dependencies tend to deprecate old functionality more smoothly, as authors are aware of the issues breaking changes cause to a package's ecosystem.

In R, the *tidyverse* bundle of packages seems ubiquitous and easy to use, but it leads to quite a few dependencies. The data.table ecosystem might be less popular but provides its functionality with a single R package dependency (the {methods} package).

Often it does not take much to get rid of dependency:

```r
library(stringr)
cow <- "A cow sounds off: mooooo"
str_extract(cow,"moo+")
```

```
[1] "mooooo"
```

Sure, the above code is more intuitive, but shrewd use of good ol' *gsub* and back-referencing allows you to do the very same thing in base R.

```r
gsub("(.+)(mooo+)","\\2",cow)
```

```
[1] "mooooo"
```

Again, {stringr} (Hadley Wickham 2022b) is certainly a well-crafted package, and it is definitely not the worst of all packages. But when you just loaded a package because it adds convenience to one single line or worse just because you found your solution online, think again before adding more dependencies to a production environment.

3.2.5 Folder Structure

In R, packages may have the following folders. Note that this does not mean a package has to contain all of these folders. FWIW, an R package, needs to have NAMESPACE and DESCRIPTION files, but that is not the point here. Also, there are more comprehensive, better books on the matter than this little section. The point of this section though is to discuss the role of folders and how they help you structure your work, even if you don't want to create an R package in the first place.

This chapter describes the role of different folders in a package and what these folders are good for. More likely than not, this will cover a lot of the aspects of your project, too.

- R
- data
- docs
- vignettes
- src
- inst
- man

The below description explains the role of all of these folders.

R

The *R* folder stores function definitions as opposed to function calls. Typically every function goes into a separate file. Sometimes, it makes sense to group multiple functions into a single file when functions are closely related. Another reason for putting more than one function into a single file is when you have a collection of relatively simple, short helper functions. The R folder **must not** contain calls[9].

```
my_func_def <- function(param1, param2){
  # here goes the function body, i.e.,
  # what the function does
  a <- (param1 + param2) * param3
  # Note that in R, return statements are
  # not necessary and even
  # relatively uncommon, R will return
  # the last unassigned statement
```

---

[9]Essentially, examples are calls, too. Note, I do recommend adding examples. Hadley Wickham's guide to documenting functions within packages (H. Wickham 2015) shows how to add examples correctly.

```
    return(a)
}
```

man

This folder contains the context manual of your package. What you'll find here is the so-called *function reference*, basically a function and dataset-specific documentation. It's what you see when you run **?function_name**. The content of the **man/** folder is usually created automatically from the *Roxygen* style documentation (note the #' styled comments) during a 'devtools::document()' run. Back in the days when people wore pijamas and lived life slow, the man folder was filled up manually with some LaTeX reminiscent .rd files, but ever since R Studio took over in 2012, most developers use *Roxygen* and render the function reference part of the documentation from their comments.

```
#' Sum of Parameters Multiplied by First Input
#'
#' This functions only exists as a show case.
#' It's useless but nevertheless exported
#' to the NAMESPACE of this
#' package so users can see it and
#'  call the function by it's name.
#'
#' @param param1 numeric input
#' @param param2 numeric input
#' @export
my_func_def <- function(param1, param2){
  # here goes the function body, i.e.,
  # what the function does
  a <- (param1 + param2) * param1
  # Note that in R, return statements are
  # not necessary and even
  # relatively uncommon, R will return
  # the last unassigned statement
```

```
    return(a)
  }
```

docs

This folder is typically not filled with content manually. When pushed to GitHub a docs folder can easily be published as website using Github Pages[10]. With GitHub Pages you can host a decently styled modern website for free. Software projects often use GitHub Pages to market a product or project or simply for documentation purposes. All you need to do is check a couple of options inside the Github Web GUI and make sure the docs/ folder contains .md or .html files as well as stylesheets (.css). The latter may sound a bit like Latin to people without a basic web development background, but there is plenty of help. The R ecosystem offers different flavors of the same idea: use a bit of markdown + R to generate website code. There is the {blogdown} R package (Xie, Hill, and Thomas 2017) for your personal website or blog. There is {pkgdown} (Hadley Wickham, Hesselberth, and Salmon 2022) for your packages documentation. And there is even bookdown to write an online book like this. Write the Markdown file, render it as HTML into the docs folder and push the docs folder to GitHub. Done. Your website will be online at username.github.io/reponame. Here is a an example of a {pkgdown} website:

https://mbannert.github.io/timeseriesdb/

data

If you have file-based data like .csv, .RData, .json or even .xlsx, put them in here. Keeping data in a separate folder inside the project directory helps to keep reference to the data relative. There is nothing more novice than `read.csv("C:\mbannert\My Documents\some_data.csv")`. Even if you like this book, I doubt you have a folder named 'mbannert' on your computer. Ah, and in case you wondered, extensive use of `setwd()` is even worse. Keep your reference to data (and functions alike) relative. If you

---

[10]https://pages.github.com/

are sourcing data from a remote NAS drive as it is common at many universities, you can simply mount this drive to your folder (LTMGTFY: How to mount a network drive Windows/OSX).

> **ℹ Note**
>
> To actually bundle data into packages, I recommend to use a `data-raw` folder for data formats other than native R formats. From the raw folder, go on to process these raw files into R representations that are then stored in `data`. The {usethis} R package (Hadley Wickham et al. 2023) is a modern boilerplate approach and suggest a smooth packaging workflow.

vignettes

Admittedly not the most intuitive names for a folder that is supposed to contain articles. Vignettes are part of the documentation of a good package. It's kind of a description as if you were to write a paper about your package, including some examples of how to use it. For modern packages, vignettes are often part of their package down based online documentation. Feel free, to name this folder differently, though sticking to the convention will make it easier to turn your project into a project at a later stage. This folder typically contains Markdown or RMarkdown files.

src

The source folder is just here for the sake of completeness and is not needed in projects that only involve R source code. It's reserved for those parts of a package that need compilation, e.g., C++ or Fortran source code.

inst

When you install an R package using `install.packages()` it will be installed in some deep dungeon on your computer where R lives within your OS. The `inst/` folder allows you to ship non-R files with your installation. The files of the inst folder will just be copied into the package root folder inside your installation of that package.

inst is also a great place to store experimental function calls or playground files once the package ambitions become more concrete, and those type of files do not live conveniently in the project root anymore. Also, I sometimes put Shiny apps for local use into the `inst/` folder if I want to make them part of a package.

3.3   Naming Conventions: Snake, Camel or Kebab Case

Let me drop a quick and general note on naming. As in how to name files, folders and functions. It may look like a mere detail, but concise formatting and styling of your code will be appreciated by your peers and by those you ask for help. Plus, following an established convention will not make you look like a complete novice.

- Do not use spaces in folder or file names! Never. If you need lengthy descriptions, use underscores '_', dashes'-' or camelCase.

- Avoid umlauts and special characters. Encoding and internationalization is worth a book of its own. It's not like modern programming environments can't handle it, but encoding will introduce further complications. These are exactly the type of complications that may lead to an unplanned, frustrating waste of hours. You may be lucky enough to find a quick fix, but you may as well not. Avoid encoding issues if you do not plan to build a deeper understanding of encoding on the fly. This is especially true for cross-platform collaborations (Windows vs. Unix/OSX).

- either go for camelCase, snake_case or kebab-case. Otherwise, prefer lower-case characters. Also make sure to not switch styles within a project. There a plenty of style guides around, go with whatever your lab or community goes.

3.4   Testing

One of the things that help scientists and business analysts reach
the next level in programming is to develop an understanding of
testing the way software engineers use the term. The colloquial
understanding of testing basically comes down to doing a couple
of dry runs before using code in production. Looking at tests
as a systematic and standardized procedure manifested in code
substantially improves the quality and reliability of one's code.

When writing software for statistical analysis, testing mostly refers
to unit tests. Unit tests are expectations expressed in code often
using a testing framework to help define expectations. In R the
{testthat} (Hadley Wickham 2011) or {tinytest} R packages (van
der Loo 2020) are examples of such frameworks.

```r
# the function
cow <- function(){

  sound_of_a_cow <- "moo"
  sound_of_a_cow

}


# A test that uses the
# testthat package to formulate
# and check expectations
library(testthat)
test_that("The cow still mooos...", {
  expect_gte(nchar(cow()),3)
  expect_true(grepl("^m",cow()))
})
```

Test passed

The above dummy function simply returns a character. The accom-
panying test checks whether the "moo" of the cow is loud enough

(=has at least 3 characters) and whether it starts with "m" (so it's not a "woof"). Note how tests typically come in bunches to thoroughly test functionality.

So why don't we write code correctly in the first place instead of writing code to check everything that could eventually go wrong? When developing *new* features, we might be confident that newly introduced features do not break existing functionality. At least until we test it :) . Experience proves that seemingly unrelated edits do cause side effects. That is why well-maintained packages have so-called unit tests that are run when the package is rebuilt. If one of the checks fails, the developer can take a look before the a change that broke the code is actually deployed. To foster the development of these type of tests, there are unit testing frameworks for many languages and frameworks.

Hadley's book *R packages* (H. Wickham 2015) has a more thorough introduction to testing in R with the {testthat} (Hadley Wickham 2011) package. Though the book is focused on R, its introduction to formal testing is very illustrative for anyone interested to add testing to their development routine.

3.5   Debugging

In programming, there is no way around debugging. From copy&paste artists to the grandmasters of hacking: writing code implies the need to debug. One of the main differences between amateur and professional is the degree to which the hunt for errors, a.k.a. bugs, is done systematically. This section gives a few tips to help organize a debugging strategy and assess how much honing of one's debugging approach is reasonable for your individual needs.

3.5.1   Read Code from the Inside Out

Many scripting languages allow some form of nesting code. In order to understand what's going on, reading and running code from innermost element first helps. Even if you are not an R user, applying the inside-out idea helps to understand what's going on. Consider the following piece of R code:

```
identical(sum(cumsum(1:10)),sum(cumsum(rev(1:10))))
```

```
[1] FALSE
```

The re-formatted version below helps to identify the innermost part of the code immediately:

```
identical(
  sum(
      cumsum(1:10)
    ),
  sum(
    cumsum(
      rev(1:10)
      )
    )
  )
```

To understand the above demo code, let's take a closer look at the innermost element(s). Also consider looking at the single function's documentation, e.g., *?rev*:

```
1:10
```

```
[1]  1  2  3  4  5  6  7  8  9 10
```

```
rev(1:10)
```

```
[1] 10  9  8  7  6  5  4  3  2  1
```

The calls to cumsum() and sum() are the next layers. Finally, identical() is the outermost function.

3.5.2 Debugger, Breakpoints, Traceback

Typically modern interpreters and/or source code editors (see chapter 4 on IDEs) provide support to make debugging more systematic. In R, you can use debug(function_name) to activate debug mode for one particular function. On the next call of function_name(), the interpreter will go through the function, executing its source line-by-line. One of the insightful things about it is that standard exploration functions like ls() list all objects within the private environment of that function (by default ls() would just list all objects within the global environment). Inspection of objects as they are seen by the functions helps to find out whether parameters are passed on correctly (or at all). Often, an error message from execution of a function motivates a debugging session. In that case, try to identify the line that causes the error and just do all the object inspection right before the line that causes the crash.

Another, similar approach is to use breakpoints which are a feature of your editor. You can activate a break point to set execution of a function to debug mode by clicking next to a line in the source of the function that should trigger the switch to debug mode. Breakpoints may be the more convenient version of using the debug tool 'per pedes' as described above because of its ability to follow function dispatch across multiple (wrapper) functions. Consider the following demo function:

```
debug_me <- function(a,b){
  out <- list()
  out$add <- a + b
  out$prod <- a * b
  out$dev <- a / b
  out$sub <- a - b
  out
}

debug_me(1,2)
```

```
$add
[1] 3

$prod
[1] 2

$dev
[1] 0.5

$sub
[1] -1
```

Now let's give this function a bad argument. (Unlike Python, R's addition operation will not simply concatenate strings when facing string input.)

```
debug_me("1","2")
# if evaluated this would return
Error in a + b : non-numeric argument
to binary operator
```

Motivated by this error message, let's switch into debug mode

```
debug(debug_me)
```

The below screenshot shows line-by-line execution of our demo function. The highlighted line marks the line which will be executed on the next press of the return key. R's debug mode can be stopped by either executing the erroneous line or by executing a capital Q command in the R console window.

```
Function: debug_me (.GlobalEnv)                    (Read-only)   ⇐≣ Next  ↑⁾ ⇐⁼  ▶ Continue   ■ Stop
  1 ▾ function(a,b){                                             > debug(debug_me)
  2      out <- list()                                          > debug_me("1","2")
⇒ 3      out$add <- a + b                                       debugging in: debug_me("1", "2")
  4      out$prod <- a * b                                      debug at #1: {
  5      out$dev <- a / b                                           out <- list()
  6      out$sub <- a - b                                           out$add <- a + b
  7      out                                                        out$prod <- a * b
  8 ▴ }                                                             out$dev <- a/b
                                                                    out$sub <- a - b
                                                                    out
                                                               }
                                                               Browse[2]>
                                                               debug at #2: out <- list()
                                                               Browse[2]>
                                                               debug at #3: out$add <- a + b
                                                               Browse[2]>
```

3.6   A Word on Peer Programming

Peer programming, also called pair programming, just means that two developers sit in front of the same screen to collaborate on a piece of code. So why is there such a buzz about it? Why is there even a term for it? And why is there a section in an applied book on it?

That is because novice programmers (and their scientific supervisors) often doubt the efficiency of two paid persons working at the same workstation. But programming is not about digging a hole with two shovels. Particularly not when it comes to building the software basis or frame of a project.

Working together using one single keyboard and screen or the virtual equivalent thereof can be highly efficient. The virtual equivalent, i.e., in fact, using two computers but sharing the screen while in call, helps tremendously with (a) your concept, (b) your documentation. Plus, it is a code review at the same time. But most importantly, both developers learn from each other. Having to explain and being challenged, deepens the understanding of experienced developers and ruthlessly identifies holes in one's knowledge. One important advice when peer programming is to switch the driver's seat from time to time. Make sure the lesser programmer holds the keys occasionally and maneuvers through articles, repositories, code and data. Doing so prevents the co-pilot from taking a back seat and letting the veteran do the entertainment. Visual Studio Code Live Share[11] is a great feature for next-level virtual peer programming, as it allows for two drivers using two cursors.

Of course, there are downsides of the pair programming approach, too. Also, timing within the lifecycle of a project is an important factor and not every project is the same fit for this agile method. But given there are so many approaches, I will leave the back and forth to others. The goal of this section is to point the reader to a practical approach that tends to work well in programming with data setups in social sciences. Googlers Jeff Dean and Sanjay Ghemawat had their fair share of success, too, according to *The New Yorker's* The Friendship That Made Google Huge[12].

---

[11]https://visualstudio.microsoft.com/services/live-share/

[12]https://www.newyorker.com/magazine/2018/12/10/the-friendship-that-made-google-huge

4

Interaction Environment

As a kid of the 90s, reading about a new editor or fancy shell coming out triggers playing Inspector Gadget's tune in my head. To invest a few fun hours into exploring a new tool that might save me a split second or two in processes that I run a hundred times daily may not always pay off by the hour even in a lifetime of programming, but it is totally worth it in most cases – at least to me. Repetitive work is tiring and error-prone, adds to cognitive workload, and shifts focus away from hard-to-tackle puzzles.

That being said, I am nowhere near the *vim* aficionados whose jaw-dropping editing speed probably takes thousands of hours to master and configure, and I would not advise overengineering setting up your environment. Like often, finding a personal middle ground between feeling totally uncomfortable outside graphical user interfaces and editing code at a 100 words per minute is key.

Most likely, investing in an initial setup of a solid editor plus some basic terminal workflows are a good starting point that can be revisited every once in a while, e.g., when we start a larger new project. What editor you will center your environment around will depend a lot on the programming language you choose. Yet, it also depends on your personal preference of how much investment, support and supportive features you want. The following features/criteria are likely the most influential when composing a programming environment for statistical computing:

- *code highlighting*, i.e., use of colors to highlight the structure of your code
- *linting* scans the code for potential errors and displays hints in the editor

Figure 4.1: Wizard or carpenter? What degree of toolset proficiency is sufficient to become happy with a programming approach to analytics? (Source: own illustration.)

- integrated *debuggers* allow running parts of the code line-by-line and to inspect the inner workings of functions
- *multi-language support* is important when working in multiple programming or markup languages.
- *terminal integration* helps to run stuff using system commands
- git integration helps interact with git and do basic add, commit, push operations through the editor's GUI
- build tools for programs that need rendering and compilation
- customizable through add-ins/macros

4.1 Integrated Development Environments

While some prefer lightning-fast editors such as Sublime Text that are easy to customize but rather basic out-of-the-box, Integrated Development Environments (IDEs) are the right choice for most people. In other words, it's certainly possible to move a five-person family into a new home by public transport, but it is not convenient.

The same holds for (plain) text editors in programming. You can use them, but most people would prefer an IDE just like they prefer to use a truck over public transport when they move. IDEs are tailored to the needs and idiosyncrasies of a language, some working with plugins and covering multiple languages. Others have a specific focus on a single language or a group of languages.

The below sections will focus on data science' most popular editors, namely Visual Studio Code and RStudio. Hence, I would like to mention at least some IDE juggernauts here, for the reader looking for alternatives: Eclipse (mostly Java but tons of plugins for other languages), or JetBrains' IntelliJ (Java) and PyCharm (Python).

4.1.1 RStudio

Posit's *RStudio* has become the default environment for most R people and those who mostly use R but C or Python and Markdown, in addition. The open source version ships for free as RStudio Desktop and RStudio Server Open Source. In addition, the creators of RStudio offer commercially supported versions of both the desktop and server version (Posit Workbench). If you want your environment to essentially look like the environment of your peers, RStudio is a good choice. To have the same visual image in mind can be very helpful in workshops, coaching or teaching.

RStudio has four control panes which the user can fill with a different functionality like script editor, R console, terminal, file explorer, environment explorer, test suite, build suite and many others. I advise newcomers to change the default to have the script editor and the console next to each other (instead of below each other). That is because (at least in the Western world) we read from left to right and send source code from left to right to execute it in the console. Combine this practice with the *run selection shortcut* (cmd+enter or ctrl+enter on a PC) and you have gained substantial efficiency compared to leaving your keyboard, reaching for your mouse and finding the right button. In addition, this workflow should allow you to see larger chunks[1] of your code as well as your output.

Explore Extensions

- explore add-ins

- explore the API

Favorite Shortcuts

- use cmd+enter (ctrl+enter on PCs) to send selected code from the script window (on the left) to the console (on the right)

- cmd+shift+option+R, while the cursor is within a function's body (create a Roxygen documentation skeleton)

- use ctrl 1,2 to switch between console and script pane

Pitfalls

- you may stumble over RStudio's defaults, such as storing your global environment on exit and thus resurrecting long forgotten objects impacting your next experiment through, e.g., lexical scoping.
- RStudio's git integration abstracts git essentials away, so it hampers understanding of what's going on.

For R, the Open Source Edition of RStudio Desktop is the right choice for most people. (If you are working in a team, R Studio's server version is great. It allows having a centrally managed server which clients can use through their web browser without even installing R and RStudio locally.) R Studio has solid support for a few other languages often used together with R, plus it's customizable. The French premier thinkR Colin_Fay gave a nice tutorial on Hacking RStudio at the useR! 2019 conference.

Back in fall 2020, long before RStudio turned into Posit, the company already indicated that data science was not about R

---

[1]Many coding conventions recommend having no more than 80 characters in one line of code. Sticking to this convention should prevent cutting off your code horizontally.

vs. **Python to them** (Remember the first section of Chapter 3 of this book: *The Choice That Doesn't Matter* of this book?)

Figure 4.2: Called RStudio back then, the company called Posit today already indicated years ago, it was not solely about R. (Source: rstudio.com website in 2021)

4.1.2 Visual Studio Code

Outside the R universe (and to some degree even inside it), Visual Studio Code became the go-to editor in data science. Microsoft's Visual Studio Code started out as a modular, general purpose IDE not focused on a single language. Meanwhile, there is not only great Python support, but also auto-completion, code highlighting for R or Julia and many other languages. VS Code Live Share is just one rather random example of its remarkably well-implemented features. Live share allows developers to edit a document simultaneously using multiple cursors similarly to Google Docs, but with all the IDE magic in a Desktop client.

4.1.3   Editors on Steroids

Another approach is to go for a highly customizable editor such as Sublime[2] or Atom[3]. The idea is to send source code from the editor to interchangeable read-eval-print-loop (REPL)s) which can be adapted according to the language that needs to be interpreted. That way a good linter/code highlighter for your favorite language is all you need to have a lightweight environment to run things. An example of such a customization approach is Christoph Sax's small project Sublime Studio[4].

For readers with Unix experience, vim[5] may just be the most ubiquitous editor of them all, to everyone else it may just live in deep nerd territory. The fact that a quick online search for "How to quit vim" came back with more than 56.4 million (!) results shows that both perspectives have a point. With vim, users can switch between a *move around* and *insert* mode. The former allows the users to use single letters as shortcuts to navigate a text file instead of typing the actual letter. This enables users to do things like move-three-words-forward or delete the next three lines and many other more complex things. Given some practice and regular use, it is easy to imagine that vim wizards can navigate their source code incredibly quickly.

Back when IDEs were less comfortable and often clunky due to their heavy lifting, a broader group of people had their incentives to invest into vim. Now that IDEs became so much better and many of them even offering vim modes or plugins, the point of contact with vim for a data scientist is mostly Unix server administration or work inside containers. GNU Emacs[6] is another noteworthy editor because, even though much more exotic, it is popular among long-tenured R folks thanks to the Emacs Speaks Statistics extension.

---

[2]https://www.sublimetext.com/
[3]https://atom.io/
[4]https://github.com/christophsax/SublimeStudio
[5]https://www.vim.org/
[6]https://www.gnu.org/software/emacs/

4.2   Notebooks

Notebooks are yet another popular choice for a home court among data scientists and analysts. Though most often associated with the Python world, notebooks are language-agnostic and also common for the R and Julia languages. The basic idea of notebooks is to run web server in the background to present a browser-based frontend to the developer. The difference between the Markdown rendering approach described in Chapter 10 about publishing is that the browser is not just used to display the result, but it is also the environment to interactively add commands. The resulting workflow, e.g., a data analysis in the making feels like a social media timeline: execute a command, receive a result posted on a web page printed below the command, again posting a prompt to expect the next command. This way we get an endless scroll of commands, analysis and descriptive text in between.

Consider the following example, drawing a basketball court using the *matplotlib* Python package. This example uses screenshots of a notebook to illustrate the difference between a notebook and concepts like RMarkdown. Note the prompts in between the results!

The above figure depicts a Markdown element in editing mode, showing the Markdown syntax (double ## for a section header of type 2). The second element is a chunk of Python code to import two well-known Python libraries.

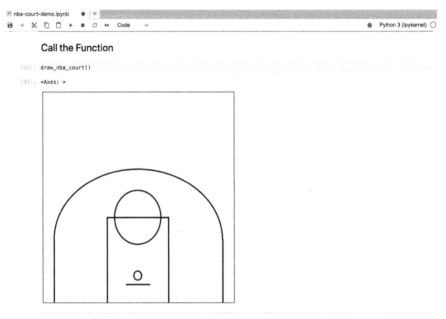

After the function definition, we see another Markdown section header element that says *Call the Function* – this time already rendered to HTML. Finally, we call the Python function defined above in another code chunk element[7].

4.3   Console/Terminal

In addition to the editor with which you will spend most of your time, it is also worthwhile to put some effort into configuring

---

[7]Though notebooks were originally designed to run on a (local) Python based webserver and to be used in a web browser, there is a neat, Electron-based standalone app called JupyterLab. I have used this app for the illustration in this book because of its slim, no-nonsense interface that unlike browsers comes without distractions from plugins.

While SSH is designed to log in to a remote server and from then on, issue commands like the server was a local Linux machine, `scp` copies files from one machine to another.

```
scp -i ~/.ssh/id_rsa ~/Desktop/a_file_on_my_desktop
  mbannert@someserver.org:/some/remote/location/
```

The above command copies a file dwelling on the user's desktop into a /some/remote/location on the server. Just like SSH, secure copy (scp) can use SSH key pair authentication, too.

4.3.2   Git Through the Console

Another common use case of the terminal is managing git . Admittedly, there is git integration for many IDEs that allows you to point and click your way to commits, pushes and pulls as well as dedicated git clients like GitHub Desktop or Source Tree. But there is nothing like the console in terms of speed and understanding what you really do. Chapter 5 sketches an idea of how to operate git through the console from the very basics to a feature branch-based workflow.

5

Git Version Control

As stated before, may be the single most important thing to take away from *Research Software Engineering* if you have not used it before. In this chapter about the way developers work and collaborate, I will stick to with *git*. The stack discussion of the previous chapter features a few more systems, but given git's dominant position, we will stick solely to git in this introduction to version control.

5.1   What Is Git Version Control?

Git is a decentralized version control system. It manages different versions of your source code (and other text files) in a simple but efficient manner that has become the industry standard: The git program itself is a small console program that creates and manages a hidden folder inside the folder you put under (you know those folders with a leading dot in their folder name, like .myfolder). This folder keeps track of all differences between the current version and other versions before the current one.

The key to appreciating the value of git is to appreciate the value of semantic versions. Git is *not* Dropbox nor Google Drive. It does *not* sync automagically (even if some Git GUI Tools suggest so). GUI tools GitHub Desktop[1], Atlassian's Source Tree[2] and Tortoise[3] are some of the most popular choices if you are not a console

---

[1]https://desktop.github.com/
[2]https://www.sourcetreeapp.com/
[3]https://tortoisegit.org/

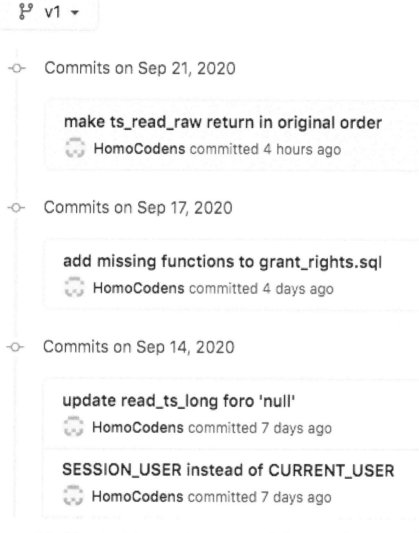

Figure 5.1: Meaningful commit messages help to make sense of a project's history. Screenshot of a commit history on GitHub. (Source: own GitHub repository.)

person. Though GUI tools may be convenient, we will use the git console throughout this book to improve our understanding. As opposed to the sync approaches mentioned above, a system allows summarizing a contribution across files and folders based on what this contribution is about. Assume you got a cool pointer from an econometrics professor at a conference, and you incorporated her advice in your work. That advice is likely to affect different parts of your work: your text and your code. As opposed to syncing each of these files based on the time you saved them, creates a version when you decide to bundle things together and to commit the change. That version could be identified easily by its commit message "incorporated advice from Anna (discussion at XYZ Conference 2020)".

5.2   Why Use Version Control in Research?

A based workflow is a path to your goals that rather consists of semantically relevant steps instead of semantically meaningless chunks based on the time you saved them.

In other, more blatant, applied words: naming files like `final_version_your_name.R` or `final_final_correction_collaboratorX_20200114.R` is like naming your WiFi `dont_park_the_car_in_the_frontyard` or `be_quiet_at_night` to communicate with your neighbors. Information is supposed to be sent in a message, not a file name. With , it is immediately clear what the most current version is, no matter the file name. There is no room for interpretation. There is no need to start guessing about the delta between the current version and another version.

Also, you can easily try out different scenarios on different branches and merge them back together if you need to. is a well-established industry standard in software development. And it is relatively easy to adopt. With datasets growing in complexity, it is only natural to improve management of the code that processes these data.

Academia has probably been the only place that would allow you to dive into hacking at somewhat complex problems for several years without ever taking notice of . As a social scientist who rather collaborates in small groups and writes moderate amount of code, have you ever thought about how to collaborate with more 100 than persons in a big software project? Or to manage 10,000 lines of code and beyond? is an important reason these things work. And it's been around for decades. But enough about the rant.

5.3 How Does Git Work?

This introduction tries to narrow things down to the commands that you'll need if you want to use git in similar fashion to what you learn from this book. If you are looking for more comprehensive, general guides, three major git platforms, namely, Atlassian's Bitbucket, GitHub and GitLab offer comprehensive introductions as well as advanced articles or videos to learn git online.

The first important implication of decentralized is that all versions are stored on the local machines of every collaborator, not just on a remote server (this is also a nice, natural backup of your work). So let's consider a single local machine first.

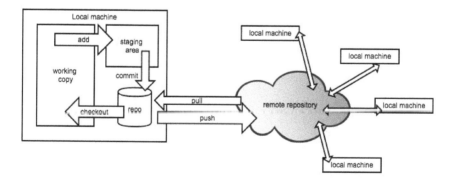

Figure 5.2: Schematic illustration of an example git workflow including remote repositories. (Source: own illustation.)

Locally, a git repository consists of a *checkout* which is also called current *working copy*. This is the status of the file that your file explorer or your editor will see when you use them to open a file. To check out a different version, one needs to call a commit by its unique commit hash and check out that particular version.

If you want to add new files to or bundle changes to some existing files into a new commit, add these files to the staging area, so they get committed next time a commit process is triggered. Finally, committing all these staged changes under another commit ID, a new version is created.

5.4   Moving Around

So let's actually do it. Here's a three-stage walk-through of git commands that should have you covered in most use cases a researcher will face. Note that git has some pretty good error messages that guess what could have gone wrong. Make sure to read them carefully. Even if you can't make sense of them, your online search will be a lot more efficient when you include these messages.

Stage 1: Working Locally

Table 5.1 summarizes essential git commands to move around your local repository.

Stage 2: Working with a Remote Repository

Though git can be tremendously useful even without collaborators, the real fun starts when working together. The first step en route to getting others involved is to add a remote repository. Table 5.2 shows essential commands for working with a remote repository.

Stage 3: Branches

Branches are derivatives from the main branch that allow to work on different features at the same time without stepping on someone else's feet. Through branches, repositories can actively maintain different states. Table 5.3 shows commands to navigate these states.

Table 5.1: Basic Commands for Working with Git

Command	Effect
git init	puts current directory and all its subdirs under version control.
git status	shows status
git add filename.py	adds file to tracked files
git commit -m "meaningful msg"	creates a new version/commit out of all staged files
git log	shows log of all commit messages on a branch
git checkout some-commit-id	goes to commit, but in detached HEAD state
git checkout main-branch-name	leaves temporary state, goes back to last commit

Table 5.2: Commands for Working with a Remote Repository

Command	Effect
git clone	creates a new repo based on a remote one
git pull	gets all changes from a linked remote repo
git push	deploys all commit changes to the remote repo
git fetch	fetches branches that were created on remote
git remote -v	shows remote repo URL
git remote set-url origin https://some-url.com	sets URL to remote repo

Table 5.3: Commands for for Handling Multiple Branches

Command	Effect
git checkout -b branchname	creates new branch named branchname
git branch	shows locally available branches
git checkout branchname	switches to branch named branchname
git switch branchname	switches to branch named branchname
git merge branchname	merges branch named branchname into current branch

Fixing Merge Conflicts

In most cases, *git* is quite clever and can figure out which is the desired state of a file when putting two versions of it together. When git's *recursive strategy* is possible, git will merge versions automatically. When the same lines were affected in different versions, git cannot tell which line should be kept. Sometimes, you would even want to keep both changes.

But even in such scenario, fixing the conflict is easy. Git will tell you that your last command caused a merge conflict and which files are conflicted. Open these files and take a look at all parts of the files in question. Figure 5.3 shows a situation in which trying merge a file that had changes across different branches caused a conflict.

Luckily, git marks the exact spot where the conflict happens. Good text editors/IDEs ship with cool colors to highlight all our options. Some of the fancier editors even have git conflict resolve plugins that let you walk through all conflict points.

At the end of the day, all do the same, i.e., remove the unwanted part, including all the marker gibberish. After you have done so, save, commit and push (if you are working with a remote repo). Don't forget to make sure you kinked out all conflicts.

```
(base) mtec-vpn-1-dhcp-0065:sandbox mbannert$ git merge a1
Updating ab22895..d762ca6
Fast-forward
 README.md | 2 ++
 1 file changed, 2 insertions(+)
(base) mtec-vpn-1-dhcp-0065:sandbox mbannert$ git merge a2
Auto-merging README.md
CONFLICT (content): Merge conflict in README.md
Automatic merge failed; fix conflicts and then commit the result.
(base) mtec-vpn-1-dhcp-0065:sandbox mbannert$
```

Figure 5.3: Ouch! We created a conflict by editing the same line in the same file on different branches. (Source: screenshot of own GitHub repository.)

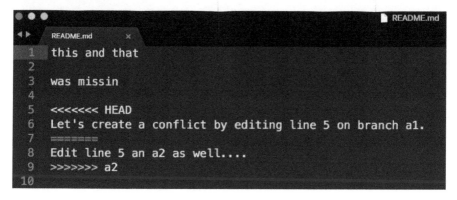

Figure 5.4: Go for the current status or take what's coming in from the a2 branch? (Source: screenshot of Sublime text editor.)

5.5 Collaboration Workflow

The broad acceptance of git as a framework for collaboration has certainly played an important role in git's establishment as an industry standard.

5.5.1 Feature Branches

This section discusses real-world collaboration workflows of modern open source software developers. Hence, the prerequisites to benefitting the most from this section are bit different. Make sure

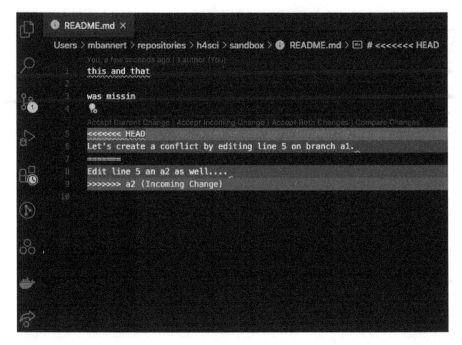

Figure 5.5: In VS Code, you can even select the option by clicking. (Source: screenshot VS Code IDE.)

you are past the mere ability to describe and explain git basics, make sure you can create and handle your own repositories.

If you had only a handful of close collaborators so far, you may be fine with staying on the main branch and trying not to step on each other's feet. This is reasonable because, git aside, it is rarely efficient to work asynchronously on exact the same lines of code anyway. Nevertheless, there is a reason why *feature-branch-based* workflows became very popular among developers: Imagine yourself collaborating in asynchronous fashion, maybe with someone in another time zone. Or with a colleague, who works on your project, but in a totally different month during the year. Or, most obviously, with someone you have never met. Forks and *feature-branch-based* workflows are the way a lot of modern open source projects tackle the above situations.

Forks are just a way to contribute via feature branches, even in case you do not have write access to a repository. But let's just have a look at the basic feature branch case, in which you are part of the team first with full access to the repository. Assume there is already some work done, some version of the project is already up on a some remote GitHub account. You join as a collaborator and are allowed to push changes now. It's certainly not a good idea to simply add things without review to a project's production. Like if you got access to modify the institute's website, and you made your first changes and all your changes go straight to production. Like this:

It used to be subtle and light gray. I swear!

Bet everybody on the team took notice of the new team member by then. In a feature branch workflow, you would start from the latest production version. Remember, git is decentralized, and you have all versions of your team's project on your local machine. Create a new branch named indicative of the feature you are looking to work on.

```
git checkout -b colorways
```

You are automatically being switched to the freshly created branch. Do your thing now. It could be just a single commit, or several commits by different persons. Once you are done, i.e., committed all changes, add your branch to the remote repository by pushing.

```
git push -u origin colorways
```

This will add your branch called *colorways* to the remote repository. If you are on any major git platform with your project, it will come with a decent web GUI. Such a GUI is the most straightforward way to do the next step: get your Pull Request (PR) out.

As you can see, git will check whether it is possible to merge automatically without interaction. Even if that is not possible, you can still issue the pull request. When you create the request, you can also assign reviewers, but you could also do so at a later stage.

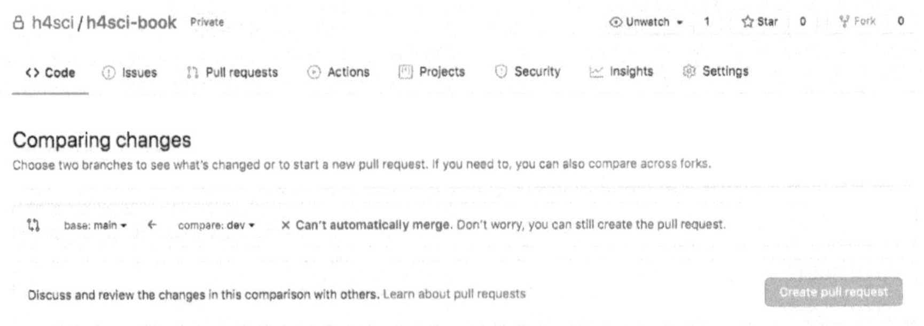

⊟ h4sci / h4sci-book Private   ⊙ Unwatch ▾ 1   ☆ Star 0   ⅄ Fork 0

<> Code   ⊙ Issues   ⇵ Pull requests   ⊙ Actions   ▣ Projects   ⊙ Security   ∿ Insights   ⊙ Settings

Comparing changes

Choose two branches to see what's changed or to start a new pull request. If you need to, you can also compare across forks.

⇵   base: main ▾   ←   compare: dev ▾   ✕ **Can't automatically merge.** Don't worry, you can still create the pull request.

Discuss and review the changes in this comparison with others. Learn about pull requests   Create pull request

Figure 5.6: GitHub Pull Request dialog: Select the *Pull Request*;
choose which branch you merge into which target branch. (Source:
own GitHub repository.)

Even after a PR was issued, you can continue to add commits to
the branch about to be merged. As long as you do not merge the
branch through the PR, commits are added to the branch. In other
words, your existing PR gets updated. This is a very natural way
to account for reviewer comments.

ℹ Note

Use commit messages like 'added join to SQLquery, closes #3'.
The keyword 'closes' or 'fixes', will automatically close issues
referred to when merged into the main branch.

Once the merge is done, all your changes are in the main branch,
and you and everyone else can pull the main branch that now
contains your new feature. Yay!

5.5.2 Pull Requests from Forks

Now, let's assume you are using an open source software created
by someone else. At some point, you miss a feature that you feel is
not too hard to implement. After googling and reading up a bit,
you realize others would like to have these features, too, but the
original authors did not find the time to implement it yet. Hence,
you get to work. Luckily, the project is open source and up on
GitHub, so you can simply get your version of it, i.e., *fork* the

project to your own GitHub account (just click the *fork* button and follow the instructions) .

Now that you have your own version of the software with all the access rights to modify it, you can implement your feature and push it to your own remote git repository. Because you forked the repository, your remote git platform will still remember where you got it from and allows you to issue a pull request to the original author. The original authors can now review the pull request, see the changes, and decide whether they are fine with the feature and its implementation.

There may very well be some back and forth in the message board before the pull requests gets merged. But usually these discussions are very context-aware and sooner or later, you will get your first pull request approved and merged. In that case, congratulations – you have turned yourself into a team-oriented open source collaborator!

5.5.3   Rebase vs. Merge

Powerful systems often provide more than one way to achieve your goals. In the case of git, putting together two branches of work – a very vital task, is exactly such a case: We can either *merge* or *rebase* branches.

While *merge* keeps the history intact, *rebase* is a history-altering command. Though most people are happy with the more straightforward *merge* approach, a bit of context is certainly helpful.

Imagine the merge approach as a branch that goes away from the trunk at some point and then grows alongside the trunk in parallel. In case both histories become out of sync because someone else adds to the main branch while you keep adding to the feature branch, you can either merge or rebase to put the two together.

Sitting on a checkout of the feature branch, a merge of the main branch would simply create an additional merge commit sequentially after the last commit of the feature branch. This merge commit contains the changes of both branches, no matter if they were automatically merged using the standard recursive strategy or through resolving a merge conflict.

As opposed to that, rebase would move all changes to main to before the feature branch started, then sequentially add all commits of the feature branch. That way your history remains linear, looks cleaner and does not contain artificial merge commits.

So, when should we merge, and when should we rebase? There is no clear rule to that other than to not use rebase on exposed branches such as main because you would have a different main branch than other developers. Rebase can ruin your collaborative workflow, yet it helps to clean up. In my opinion, merging feature branches is just fine for most people and teams. So unless you have too many people working on too many different features at once and are in danger of not being able to move through your history, simply go with the merge approach. The following Atlassian tutorial[4] offers more insights and illustrations to deepen your understanding of the matter.

---

[4]https://www.atlassian.com/git/tutorials/merging-vs-rebasing

6

Data Management

Admittedly, I have said the same thing about Chapter 5 on version control, yet *data management* may be the single most impactful chapter of this book. This may be the case in particular if you come from an environment that mostly organized data in spreadsheets shared via e-mail or network drives. To contextualize data and think about (long-term) data management is a step into a bigger world.

After decades of information engineering and computer science, some can't help wondering why we have not found one perfect, one-size-fits-all form of data. In fact, a substantial part of programming with data deals with transforming data from one form into another. This chapter intends to give an idea of the aspects of data management most relevant for data analytics. Hopefully, this chapter helps the reader to assess how far they wanted to dig into data management.

6.1 Forms of Data

In research and analytics, data appear in a plethora of different forms. Yet, most researchers and business analysts are mainly trained to handle different flavors of two-dimensional data, as in **one-observation-one-row**. Ad hoc studies conducted once result in *cross-sectional data*: one line per observation; columns represent variables. Sensor data, server logs or forecasts of official statistics are examples of single variable data observed over time. These single variable, longitudinal data are also known as *time series*. Multivariate time series, i.e., multivariable, longitudinal data are

often referred to as *panel data*. In our heads, all of these forms
of data are typically represented as rectangular, two-dimensional
one-line-per-observation, spreadsheet-like tables. Here are a few
easy-to-reproduce examples using popular R demo datasets.

```
h <- head(mtcars)
h
```

```
                   mpg cyl disp  hp drat    wt  qsec vs am gear carb
Mazda RX4          21.0   6  160 110 3.90 2.620 16.46  0  1    4    4
Mazda RX4 Wag      21.0   6  160 110 3.90 2.875 17.02  0  1    4    4
Datsun 710         22.8   4  108  93 3.85 2.320 18.61  1  1    4    1
Hornet 4 Drive     21.4   6  258 110 3.08 3.215 19.44  1  0    3    1
Hornet Sportabout  18.7   8  360 175 3.15 3.440 17.02  0  0    3    2
Valiant            18.1   6  225 105 2.76 3.460 20.22  1  0    3    1
```

```
    dim(h)
```

```
[1]  6 11
```

The above output shows an excerpt of the *mtcars* **cross-sectional**
dataset with 6 lines and 11 variables. *Airpassenger* is a **time series**
dataset represented in an R *ts* object which is essentially a vector
with time-based index attribute.

```
AirPassengers
```

```
      Jan Feb Mar Apr May Jun Jul Aug Sep Oct Nov Dec
1949 112 118 132 129 121 135 148 148 136 119 104 118
1950 115 126 141 135 125 149 170 170 158 133 114 140
1951 145 150 178 163 172 178 199 199 184 162 146 166
1952 171 180 193 181 183 218 230 242 209 191 172 194
1953 196 196 236 235 229 243 264 272 237 211 180 201
1954 204 188 235 227 234 264 302 293 259 229 203 229
1955 242 233 267 269 270 315 364 347 312 274 237 278
1956 284 277 317 313 318 374 413 405 355 306 271 306
1957 315 301 356 348 355 422 465 467 404 347 305 336
1958 340 318 362 348 363 435 491 505 404 359 310 337
1959 360 342 406 396 420 472 548 559 463 407 362 405
1960 417 391 419 461 472 535 622 606 508 461 390 432
```

Let's create **a multivariate time series (panel)** dataset, i.e.,
multiple variables observed over time:

```
d <- data.frame(Var1 = rnorm(10, 0),
                Var2 = rnorm(10, 10),
                Var3 = rnorm(10, 30))
multi_ts <- ts(d, start = c(2000,1), frequency = 4)
multi_ts
```

```
                 Var1        Var2      Var3
2000 Q1   0.12007903  10.174062  29.90658
2000 Q2  -1.47470510   9.942915  31.27412
2000 Q3   0.34821894   8.199177  29.40425
2000 Q4   0.08374196   8.388996  30.59842
2001 Q1  -0.13013678  11.605116  29.90253
2001 Q2   0.67590396   8.649748  28.71689
2001 Q3   0.48234332   7.171355  31.88178
2001 Q4  -0.87175815  11.859055  28.35145
2002 Q1   0.63129797   9.486677  30.61444
2002 Q2  -0.40774503  11.149892  29.56971
```

> **i** **A Note on Long Format vs. Wide Format** The above
> multivariable time series is shown in what the data science
> community calls *wide* format. In this most intuitive format,
> every column represents one variable, time is on the Y-
> axis. The counterpart is the so-called *long* format shown
> below. The long format is a machine-friendly, flexible way to
> represent multi-variable data without altering the number
> of columns with more variables.

```
library(tsbox)
ts_dt(multi_ts)[1:15,]
```

```
      id        time            value
1:  Var1  2000-01-01   0.12007903
2:  Var1  2000-04-01  -1.47470510
3:  Var1  2000-07-01   0.34821894
4:  Var1  2000-10-01   0.08374196
5:  Var1  2001-01-01  -0.13013678
```

```
 6: Var1 2001-04-01  0.67590396
 7: Var1 2001-07-01  0.48234332
 8: Var1 2001-10-01 -0.87175815
 9: Var1 2002-01-01  0.63129797
10: Var1 2002-04-01 -0.40774503
11: Var2 2000-01-01 10.17406248
12: Var2 2000-04-01  9.94291482
13: Var2 2000-07-01  8.19917666
14: Var2 2000-10-01  8.38899562
15: Var2 2001-01-01 11.60511599
```

The ability to transform data from one format into the other and to manipulate both formats is an essential skill for any data scientist or data engineer. It is important to point out that the ability to do the above transformations effortlessly is an absolute go-to skill for people who want to use programming to run analysis. (Different analyses or visualizations may require one form or the other and ask for quick transformation).

Hence, popular data science programming languages offer great toolsets to get the job done. Mastering these toolboxes is not the focus of this book. R for Data Science and the Carpentries are good starting points if you feel the need to catch up or solidify your know-how.

Yet, not all information suits a two-dimensional form. Handling nested or unstructured information is one of the fields where the strength of a programming approach to data analysis and visualization comes into play. Maps are a common form of information that is often represented in nested fashion. For an example of nested data[1], let's take a look at the map file and code example case study in Section 11.6. In memory, i.e., in our R session, the data is represented in a list that contains multiple list elements and may contain more lists nested inside.

---

[1]The original GeoJSON file from the example can be found at https://raw. githubusercontent.com/mbannert/maps/master/ch_bfs_regions.geojson.

```
library(jsonlite)

json_ch <- jsonlite::read_json(
  "https://raw.githubusercontent.com/...."
)
ls.str(json_ch)
```

```
crs : List of 2
 $ type      : chr "name"
 $ properties:List of 1
features : List of 7
 $ :List of 3
 $ :List of 3
 $ :List of 3
 $ :List of 3
 $ :List of 3
 $ :List of 3
 $ :List of 3
type :  chr "FeatureCollection"
```

Another example of nested but structured data is HTML or XML trees obtained from scraping websites. Typically, web scraping approaches like rvest (Hadley Wickham 2022a) or BeautifulSoup (Zheng, He, and Peng 2015) parse the hierarchical Document Object Model (DOM) and turn it into an in-memory representation of a website's DOM. For a DOM parsing example, see case study Section 11.4.

6.2 Representing Data in Files

To create the above examples of different forms of data, it was mostly sufficient to represent data in memory, in this case within an R session. As an interpreted language, an R interpreter has to run at all times when using R. The very same is true for Python. Users of these languages can work interactively, very much like with a pocket calculator on heavy steroids. All functions, all data, are in loaded into a machine's RAM (memory) represented as objects of various classes. This is convenient, but has an obvious limitation: once the sessions ends, the information is gone. Hence, we need to have a way to store at least the results of our computation in persistent fashion.

Just like in office or image editing software, the intuitive way to store data persistently from a programming language is to store data into files. The choice of the file format is much less straightforward in our case, though. The different forms of data discussed above, potential collaborators and interfaces are factors among others that weigh into our choice of a file format.

6.2.1   Spreadsheets

Based on our two-dimensional focused intuition and training, spreadsheets are the on-disk analog of data.frames, data.tables and tibbles. Formats like **.csv** or **.xlsx** are the most common way to represent two-dimensional data on disk.

On the programming side, the ubiquity of spreadsheets leads to a wide variety of libraries to parse and write different spreadsheet formats.

```
import csv
import pandas as pd

d = {'column1': [1,2], 'column2': [3,4]}
df = pd.DataFrame(data=d)
df.to_csv("an_example.csv", sep=";",encoding='utf-8')
```

Comma-separated values (.csv)[2] are a good and simple option. Their text-based nature makes .csv files language agnostic and human-readable through a text editor.

---

[2]Note that commas are not always necessarily the separator in .csv files. Because of the use of commas as decimal delimiters in some regions, columns are also often separated by semicolons to avoid conflicts.

```
;column1;column2
0;1;3
1;2;4
```

Though Excel spreadsheets are a convenient interface to office environments that offer extras such organization into workbooks, the simpler .csv format has advantages in machine-to-machine communication and as an interface between different programming languages and tools. For example, web visualization libraries such as highcharts or echarts are most commonly written in JavaScript and can conveniently consume data from .csv files. The above example .csv file was written in Python and is now easily read by R.

```
library(readr)
csv <- readr::read_csv2("an_example.csv")
csv
```

```
# A tibble: 2 x 3
   ...1 column1 column2
  <dbl>   <dbl>   <dbl>
1     0       1       3
2     1       2       4
```

6.2.2 File Formats for Nested Information

For many data engineers and developers. JavaScript Object Notation (JSON)[3] has become the go-to file format for nested data. Just like with .csv basically every programming language used in data science and analytics has libraries to serialize and deserialize JSON (read and write). Though harder to read for humans than .csv, prettified JSON with a decent highlighting color scheme is easy to read and gives the human reader a good understanding of the hierarchy at hand. The added complexity comes mostly from the nested nature of the data, not so much from the file format.

---

[3]https://json.org

```r
library(jsonlite)

li <- list(
  element_1 = head(mtcars, 2),
  element_2 = head(iris, 2)
)

toJSON(li, pretty = TRUE)
```

```json
{
  "element_1": [
    {
      "mpg": 21,
      "cyl": 6,
      "disp": 160,
      "hp": 110,
      "drat": 3.9,
      "wt": 2.62,
      "qsec": 16.46,
      "vs": 0,
      "am": 1,
      "gear": 4,
      "carb": 4,
      "_row": "Mazda RX4"
    },
    {
      "mpg": 21,
      "cyl": 6,
      "disp": 160,
      "hp": 110,
      "drat": 3.9,
      "wt": 2.875,
      "qsec": 17.02,
      "vs": 0,
      "am": 1,
      "gear": 4,
      "carb": 4,
```

```
      "_row": "Mazda RX4 Wag"
    }
  ],
  "element_2": [
    {
      "Sepal.Length": 5.1,
      "Sepal.Width": 3.5,
      "Petal.Length": 1.4,
      "Petal.Width": 0.2,
      "Species": "setosa"
    },
    {
      "Sepal.Length": 4.9,
      "Sepal.Width": 3,
      "Petal.Length": 1.4,
      "Petal.Width": 0.2,
      "Species": "setosa"
    }
  ]
}
```

The above example shows the first two lines of two different, un-related rectangular datasets. Thanks to the hierarchical nature of JSON, both datasets can be stored in the same file albeit totally different columns. Again, just like .csv, JSON works well as an interface, but it is more flexible than the former.

Besides JSON, **XML** is the most common format to represent nested data in files. Though there are a lot of overlapping use cases, there is a bit of a different groove around both of these file formats. JSON is perceived as more lightweight and close to "the web" while XML is the traditional, very explicit no-nonsense format. XML has a **Document Type Definition (DTD)** that defines the structure of the document and which elements and attributes are legal. Higher level formats use this more formal approach as XML-based definition. SDMX[4], a world-wide effort to provide a

---

[4]SDMX (https://sdmx.org) stands for Statistical Data and Metadata eXchange is an international initiative that aims at standardizing and modernizing

format for exchange statistical data and metadata, is an example of such a higher level format build on XML.

The above example shows an excerpt of the main economic forward-looking indicator (FLI) for Switzerland, the KOF Economic Barometer, represented in an SDMX XML file. Besides the value and the date index, several attributes provide the consumer with an elaborate data description. In addition, other nodes and their children provide information like *Contact* or *ID* in the very same file. Note that modern browsers often provide code folding for nodes and highlighting to improve readability.

6.2.3   A Word on Binaries

Unlike all file formats discussed above, binaries cannot be read by humans using a simple text editor. In other words, you will need the software that wrote the binary to read it again. If that software was expensive and/or exotic, your work is much less accessible, more difficult to share and harder to reproduce. Though this disadvantage of binaries is mitigated when you use freely available open source software, storing data in binaries can still be a hurdle.

But, of course, binaries do have advantages, too: binaries can compress their content and save space. Binaries can take on all sorts of in-memory objects including functions, not just datasets. In other words, binaries can bundle stuff. Consider the following load/save operation in R:

```
bogus <- function(a,b){
  a + b
}
```

("industrializing") the mechanisms and processes for the exchange of statistical data and metadata among international organizations and their member countries. SDMX is sponsored by seven international organizations including the Bank for International Settlements (BIS), the European Central Bank (ECB), Eurostat (Statistical Office of the European Union), the International Monetary Fund (IMF), the Organisation for Economic Co-operation and Development (OECD), the United Nations Statistical Division (UNSD), and the World Bank.

```
data(Airpassengers)
data(mtcars)

s <- summary(mtcars)

save("bogus", "Airpassengers","s",
    file="bundle.RData")
```

In memory, *bogus* is a *function*, Airpassengers is an R *time series* object and *s* is a *list* based summary object. All of these objects can be stored in a single binary RData file using *save()*. A fresh R session can now *load()* everything stored in that file.

```
load("bundle.RData")
```

> **i** Note
>
> Notice that unlike reading a .csv or .json file, the call does not make any assignments into a target object. This is because all objects are loaded into an R environment (*.globalEnv* by default) with their original names.

6.2.4 Interoperable File Formats

Interoperable file formats cover some middle ground between the options described above. The *cross-language in-memory development platform* Apache Arrow[5] is a well-established project that also implements file formats that work across many popular (data science) environments. Though the major contribution of the Apache Arrow project is to allow sharing in-memory data store across environments, I will just show it as an example for interoperable file formats here. Nevertheless, if you're interested in a modern, yet established cross-environment data science project, digging deeper into Apache Arrow is certainly a fun experience.

---

[5]https://arrow.apache.org/

From the Apache Arrow documentation:

```r
library(dplyr)
library(arrow)
data("starwars")
file_path_sw <- "starwars.parquet"
write_parquet(starwars, file_path_sw)
```

The above R code writes the *starwars* demo dataset from the *dplyr* R package to a temporary .parquet file. The {arrow} R package (Richardson et al. 2022) comes with the necessary toolset to write the open source columnar[6] .parquet format. Though they are not text files, .parquet files can be read and written from different environments and consume the file written with R. The below code uses the arrow library for Python to read the file we have just written with R.

```python
import pyarrow.parquet as pa
sw = pa.read_table("starwars.parquet")
print(*sw.column_names, sep="\n")
```

```
name
height
mass
hair_color
skin_color
eye_color
birth_year
sex
gender
homeworld
species
films
vehicles
starships
```

---

[6] see also

Here's Julia reading our Parquet file:

```
using Parquet
sw = Parquet.File("starwars.parquet")
```

```
Parquet file: starwars.parquet
    version: 2
    nrows: 87
    created by: parquet-cpp-arrow version 9.0.0
    cached: 0 column chunks
```

When I composed this example, reading and writing *Parquet* files in different environments, I ran into several compatibility issues. This shows that the level of interoperability is not the same as the interoperability of text files.

6.2.4.1   A Note on Overhead

The *parquet* format is designed to read and write files swiftly and to consume less disk space than text files. Both features can become particularly relevant in the cloud. Note though that *Parquet* comes with some overhead, which may eat up gains if datasets are small. Consider our *starwars* dataset. At 87 rows and 14 columns, the dataset is rather small.

```
library(readr)
write_csv(starwars, file = "starwars.csv")
dim(starwars)
```

```
[1] 87 14
```

```
round(file.size("starwars.parquet") /
      file.size("starwars.csv"),
      digits = 2)
```

```
[1] 1.47
```

Hence, the overhead of a schema implementation and other meta information outweighs *Parquet's* compression for such a small dataset, leading to a *Parquet* file that is almost 1.5 times larger than the corresponding csv file. Yet, *Parquet* already turns the tables for the *diamonds* demo dataset from the *ggplot2* R package, which is by no means a large dataset.

```
library(ggplot2)
data(diamonds)
write_csv(diamonds, file = "diamonds.csv")
write_parquet(diamonds, "diamonds.parquet" )
round(file.size("diamonds.parquet") /
      file.size("diamonds.csv"),
      digits = 2)
```

[1] 0.21

The *Parquet* file for the *diamonds* dataset has roughly one fifth of the size of the corresponding text file. This is a great example of why there is not one single, perfect, one-size-fits all form of data that emerged from decades of information engineering. So when you choose how you are going to represent data in our project, think about your goals, your most common use or query and a smooth data transformation strategy for when the use cases or goals change.

6.3 Databases

Given the options that file-based approaches provide, what is (a) the difference and (b) the added value of going for a database to manage data? The front-and-center difference is the client interface, but there are many more differences and benefits.

database users use a client program and a query language to send queries written to a database. The client sends these queries to the database host and either performs an operation on the database quietly or returns a result. The most common example of such a query language is the Structured Query Language (SQL). Using such a query language leads to a standard way of interaction with the data, no matter how the dataset looks like in terms of dimensions, size etc.SQLdatabases have been around much longer than data science itself, and continue to be inevitable as application backends and data archives for many use cases.

```
SELECT * FROM myschema.demotable
```

The above query would return all rows and all columns from a table called *demotable* in a schema called *myschema*. Such a query can easier be sent from a standalone database client, a database specific IDE with a built in client such as DataGrip[7] or a programming language. Given the ubiquity of databases most basically any programming language has native interfaces to the most common database. And if that is not the case, there is the database management system agnostic ODBC standard that is supported by all majorSQLdatabases. The below code shows how to connect from R to PostgreSQL, send queries from within R and receive results as R objects.

```
library(RPostgres)
con <- dbConnect(
  host = "localhost",
  user = "bugsbunny",
  # only works within RStudio
  passwd = .rs.AskForPassword("Enter Pw"),
  dbname = "some_db_name"
)

# the result is an R data.frame
res <- dbSendQuery(con,
  "SELECT * FROM myschema.demotable")

# and we can do R things with it
# such as show the first 6 lines.
```

---

[7]https://www.jetbrains.com/datagrip/

```
head(res)
dbDisconnect(con)
```

Obviously, the above example barely shows the tip of the iceberg, as it is just meant to illustrate the way we interact with databases as opposed to a file system. To dig a little deeper into databases, I recommend getting a solid understanding of the basic CREATE, SELECT, INSERT, UPDATE, DELETE, TRUNCATE, DROP processes as well as basic JOINs and WHERE clauses. Also, it is helpful to understand the concept of normalization up to the third normal form.

Figure 6.1: The iconic Postgres elephant logo.

6.3.1 Relational database Management Systems (RDBMS)

When you need to pick a concrete database technology for your project, the first major choice is whether to go for a relational system or not. Unless you have a very compelling reason not to, you are almost always better off with a relational database: Relational databases are well established and accessible from any programming language used in programming with data that one could think of. In addition, modern RDBMS implementations offer many non-relational features such as JSON field types and operations.

I would classify the most popular relational database implementations as follows. First, there is SQLite. As the name suggestions,

SQLite is a light-weight, stripped down, easy-to-use and install implementation.

> SQLite is a C-language library that implements a small, fast, self-contained, high-reliability, full-featured,SQLdatabase engine. SQLite is the most used database engine in the world. SQLite is built into all mobile phones and most computers and comes bundled inside countless other applications that people use every day. – SQLite.org

SQLite data lives in a single file that the user queries through the *SQLite* engine. Here is an example using that engine from R.

```
library(RSQLite)
db_path <- "rse.sqlite3"
con <- dbConnect(RSQLite::SQLite(), db_path)
dbWriteTable(con, dbQuoteIdentifier(con,"mtcars"),
             mtcars, overwrite = T)
dbWriteTable(con, dbQuoteIdentifier(con,"flowers"),
             iris, overwrite = T)
```

The above code initiates a *SQLite* database and continues to write the built-in R demo datasets into separate tables in that newly created database. Now we can useSQLto query the data. Return the first three rows of *flowers*:

```
dbGetQuery(con, "SELECT * FROM flowers LIMIT 3")
```

```
  Sepal.Length Sepal.Width Petal.Length Petal.Width Species
1          5.1         3.5          1.4         0.2  setosa
2          4.9         3.0          1.4         0.2  setosa
3          4.7         3.2          1.3         0.2  setosa
```

Return cars that are more fuel efficient than 30 miles per gallon:

```
dbGetQuery(con, "SELECT * FROM mtcars WHERE mpg > 30")
```

```
   mpg cyl disp  hp drat    wt  qsec vs am gear carb
1 32.4   4 78.7  66 4.08 2.200 19.47  1  1    4    1
2 30.4   4 75.7  52 4.93 1.615 18.52  1  1    4    2
3 33.9   4 71.1  65 4.22 1.835 19.90  1  1    4    1
4 30.4   4 95.1 113 3.77 1.513 16.90  1  1    5    2
```

MySQL[8] can do a little more and is also immensely popular, particularly as a database backend for web content management systems and other web-based applications. The so-called LAMP stack (Linux, Apache, MySQL and PHP) contributed to its rise decades ago when it fueled many smaller and medium-level web projects around the world. In its early days, MySQL used to be an independent open source project, but it was later on acquired by database Juggernaut Oracle as a light version to go with its flagship product.

While certainly doing its job in millions of installations, MySQL is not in at the same level as [Microsoft SQL Server[9] (MSSQL), PostgreSQL[10] and Oracle database[11], and I suggest one of these three enterprise-level databases as a data store for research projects that go beyond hosting a blog. Especially when it comes to long-term conservation of data and enforcing consistency, MSSQL, PostgreSQL and Oracle are hard to beat. Among the three, personally I would always lean toward the license cost free open source PostgreSQL, but fitting into existing ecosystems is a good reason to go with either MSSQL or Oracle if you can afford the licenses. For many use cases, there is hardly any difference for the analyst or scientific end user. PostgreSQL may have the coolest spatial support, MSSQL T-SQL dialect, may have some extra convenient queries if your developers mastered the dialect and Oracle may have the edge in performance and Java interaction here and there, but none of these systems is a bad choice.

Another database management that gets a lot of attention recently (and rightfully so) is DuckDB[12]. Because it is mentioned so positively and often, it is important to understand what it is and when to use it. DuckDB is not yet another competitor that tries to gain some ground from the big three of MSSQL, PostgreSQL and Oracle. DuckDB does offer an SQL interface, but it is very different in its aims from the traditionalSQLdatabases. DuckDB is serverless and

---

[8]https://www.mysql.com/

[9]https://www.microsoft.com/en-us/sql-server/sql-server-2019

[10]https://www.postgresql.org/

[11]https://www.oracle.com/database/technologies/

[12]https://duckdb.org/

allows accessing *Parquet* files via a very fast SQL interface. This makes DuckDB a great tool for interactive analysis and transfer of large result sets, but it is not so suitable for enterprise data warehousing.

6.3.2 A Word on Non-Relational databases

Among other things, relational databases are ACID (Atomicity, Consistency, Isolation, and Durability) compliant and ask for very little in return to provide us with a framework to keep our data quality high for decades. So unless, you have a very specific use case that translates to a compelling reason to use a non-relational database stick to SQL. Document-oriented storage or very unstructured information could be such a reason to use non-relational databases, yet their JSON support allows to also handle JSON in database cells. About a decade ago, mongoDB[13] gained traction, partly piggybacking the success of JavaScript and server-side JavaScript in particular. In web development, the MEAN (mongoDB, expressjs, angular and node) stack become popular, and, with the bundle, the idea of non-relational databases as fast track to a backend spread.

Columnar stores, which are also considered non-relational, are conceptionally similar to relational databases, though denormalized and designed to structure sparse data. database systems like Apache Cassandra[14] are designed to scale horizontally and be highly available, managing massive amounts of data. Cloud applications that distribute data across multiple nodes for high availability benefit from such an approach. Other options include Redis[15] or Couchbase[16]. If you are not happy with the "beyond-the-scope-of-this-book" argument, blogging experts like Lukas Eder[17] maybe biased but much better educated (and fun) to educate you here.

---

[13]https://www.mongodb.com/
[14]https://cassandra.apache.org/
[15]https://redis.io/
[16]https://www.couchbase.com/
[17]https://blog.jooq.org/tag/nosql/

6.4   Non-Technical Aspects of Managing Data

The fact that we can do more data work single-handedly than ever before does not only equate to more options. It also means we need to be aware of new issues and responsibilities. Those responsibilities range from leading by example when it comes to etiquette and ethical aspects, to sticking to privacy rules and complying with security standards. In addition, to normative restrictions that come with handling data, the options and choices of data dissemination are a realm of their own. Just like software publications, you should not just "drop" data without a license and instructions on acceptable use of the data.

6.4.1   Etiquette

Just because content is publicly available on a website does not automatically mean that bulk downloads, aggregation and republishing are ok. For example, the ability to scrape a website daily and doing so with good intent for science does not mean a website's Acceptable Use Policy (AUP) allows to systematically archive its content.

> **!** Be responsible when scraping data from websites by following polite principles: introduce yourself, ask for permission, take slowly and never ask twice. – CRAN description of the {polite} R package (Perepolkin 2023).

In other words, the new type of researcher discussed in this book needs to be aware of potential legal and social consequences. The {polite} R package quoted above is an example of an alternative approach that favors etiquette over hiding IP addresses to avoid access denial.

6.4.2 Security

> I ain't got nothing to hide. I don't care about people reading
> my stuff. – an argument I have heard about a zillion times.

People who argue like that do not only endanger their environment, they also contribute to a less secure internet at large, as they leave their device open to contribute to malicious activity. It does not have to be you who has been trusted to work with data that qualify as sensitive. Someone on your team or within your network might have been, and that person may trust you more than a stranger and may be less vigilant when harmful actions are executed in your name. This is why you are *obliged* to care about security. As in, do *not* store your credentials in your scripts. As in, passwords are *not* part of your analysis. You may accidentally push your password to GitHub, where it is not only publicly available but also hard to truly delete for beginners. Make sure to choose secure passwords. Use a password manager, so the passwords do not need to be your cat's name for you to remember. Also, with a password manager you can afford *not* to have the same passwords for multiple applications. Use a password manager so you can afford to change your passwords. Use key files where you can. The case study chapter gives you a hands-on recipe to use RSA key pairs to connect to remote servers, e.g., your GitHub account instead of a username/password combination. This is also a good way to connect to a remote server via SSH.

In addition to the above Brainy Smurf advice, let me mention security as a reason to consider using a database to manage and archive your data for the long haul. Enterprise-level databases allow for granular access management and help to stay ahead of users and their rights regarding your database's entries.

6.4.3 Privacy

Privacy in data science is a complex issue and could legitimately fill a book on its own. Though I cannot comprehensively cover privacy in a section, it is important to me to raise awareness and hopefully create an entry point to the matter. When working with data, in its essence, respecting privacy is about avoiding exposure of individual units without their explicit prior consent. It is important to understand that exposure does not stop at names. A single extraordinary feature or an exotic combination of features can identify an individual within a dataset, or at least expose a group. This is why merging multiple datasets may also cause privacy concerns when datasets were not created to be merged in the first place, and/or individuals were not aware that merging was possible. So, what can we as researchers learn from here, except from concerns and further complication of our work? First, licenses and usage policies are a service to users of the data. Second, awareness of what is sensitive data is a valuable skill to have on a team. That being said, management of in-depth knowledge is rather easy to organize in a centralized fashion. Most universities and larger corporations will have an officer to run these things by.

6.4.4   Data Publications

Yet, there is more to managing your data's exposure than just making sure everything is encrypted and locked up. Publication of data makes your results reproducible and improves trust in said results. As a consequence, there is a notable crescendo in the claim for reproducible research. While reproducible research is great, I would like to raise awareness that essentially all solutions created and advertised to improve reproducibility implicitly assume the researcher deals with datasets obtained through a study. In other words, it is implied that your work is not about monitoring an ongoing process.

Data Archives

Research repositories like Zenodo[18] that allow to archive data follow a snapshot thinking: A catalog entry refers to a particular version of an research paper, report, software or dataset. Whenever there is an update, a new version is added to a catalog entry. Adding datasets or software publications to catalogs like Zenodo does not only improve reproducibility, it also helps data workers get credit

---

[18]https://zenodo.org

for their contribution. Fortunately, feeding research repositories is a task that is easy to automate thanks to great integration, APIs and community work.

Open Data

Open Data archives are a special form of repositories. The term "open data" refers to publicly available data that are available free of license costs and in machine-readable fashion.

> Open data and content can be freely used, modified, and shared by anyone for any purpose – opendefinition.org

Because of approaches such as the Swiss government's "open by default," open government data (OGD) has become a common form of open data. The basic idea that data generated from publicly funded processes should be publicly available whenever no privacy rights are violated has been the motor for many OGD projects out of public administration. From small local governments to international organizations like the World Bank or OECD, open data have become a valuable and growing source for researchers. Open data initiatives of your country, as well as major international organizations, will help you to create interoperable datasets. In addition, open data organizations provide you with a publication channel for your data or with a data catalog that stores the data description. Initiatives like SDMX (Statistical Data and Meta eXchange)[19] aim to improve exchange of data *and* data descriptions. Their XML-based format has become an international standard which led to the implementation of SDMX read and write routines in statistical software. Whether you think about the conditions of your own data publications or about a source for your own research project, make sure to consider open data.

> *openwashdata* is an active global community that applies FAIR principles to data generated in the greater water, sanitation, and hygiene (WASH) sector – openwashdata.org

The *openwashdata* project I have been contributing to might be an hands-on inspiration to get a more concrete understanding of what

---

[19]https://sdmx.org/

open data is actually about. Among other things, the openwashdata project collects datasets from publications and republishes them in machine readable format alongside their meta information. The data manipulation to reach this end is documented in reproducible fashion. The final results, R data packages, are published in freely available git repositories in the project's GitHub organization.

7

Infrastructure

Yes, there is a third area besides your research and carpentry-level programming that I suppose you should get an idea about. Again, you do not have to master hosting servers or even clusters, but a decent overview and an idea of when to use what will help you tremendously to plan ahead. The Figure 7.1 shows a simple web application setup that would work well with virtual machines as well as with docker containers.

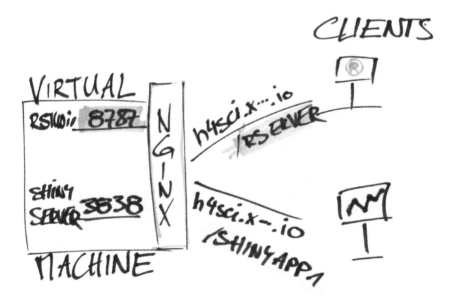

Figure 7.1: Schematic illustration of a simple server setup for web-based IDE and web application server. (Source: own illustration.)

7.1 Why Go Beyond a Local Notebook?

Admittedly, unless you just always had a knack for Arduinos, Raspberry Pis or the latest beta version of the software you use, infrastructure may be the one area you perceive as distracting, none-of-your-business overhead. So, why leave the peaceful, well-known shire of our local environment for the uncharted, rocky territory of unwelcoming technical documentations and time-consuming rabbit holes?

Figure 7.2: Though servers can provide access to massive computing resources, do not think of them as a data vault that looks like a fridge. (Source: own illustration.)

Performance, particularly in terms of throughput, is one good reason to look beyond desktop computers. Data protection regulations that prohibit data downloads may simply force us to not work locally. Or we just do not want a crashing office application to bring down a computation that ran for hours or even days. Or we need a computer that is online 24/7 to publish a report, website or data visualization.

Figure 7.3: Think of a server as a "program that listens". (Source: own illustration.)

7.2   Hosting Options

So, where should we go with our project when it outgrows the local environment of our notebooks? This has actually become a tough question because of all the reasonable options out there. Technical advances, almost unparalleled scalability and large profits for the biggest players made modern infrastructure providers offer an incredible variety of products to choose from. Obviously, a description of product offerings in a vastly evolving field is not well suited for discussions in a book. Hence, *Research Software Engineering* intends to give an overview to classify the general options and common business models.

7.2.1   Software-as-a-Service

The simplest solution and fastest time-to-market is almost always to go for a Software-as-a-Service (SaaS) product – particularly if you are not experienced in hosting and just want to get started without thinking about which Linux to use and how to maintain your server. SaaS products abstract all of that away from the user and focus on doing one single thing well. The shinyapps.io[1] platform is a great example of such a service: users can sign up and deploy their web applications within minutes. The shinyapps.io platform is a particularly interesting example of a SaaS product because R developers who come from field-specific backgrounds other than programming are often not familiar with web development and hosting websites. Some of these developers, for whom R might be their first programming language, are suddenly empowered to develop and run online content thanks to the R Shiny web application framework that uses R to generate HTML, CSS and JavaScript based applications. Still, those applications need to be hosted somewhere. This is precisely what shinyapps.io does. The service solely hosts web applications that were created with the Shiny web application framework. This ease of use is also the biggest limitation of SaaS products. A website generated with another tool

---

[1]https://shinyapps.io

cannot be deployed easily. In addition, the mere bang-for-buck price is rather high compared to self-hosting as users pay for a highly, standardized, managed hosting product. Nevertheless, because of the low volume of most projects, SaaS is feasible for many projects, especially at a proof of concept stage.

> **i** In case you are interested in getting started with Shiny, take a look at the Shiny case study in this book. The study explains basic concepts of Shiny to the user and walks readers through the creation and deployment of a simple app.

SaaS, of course, is neither an R nor a data science idea. Modern providers offer databases, storage calendars, face recognition and location services, among other things.

7.2.2 Self-Hosted

The alternative approach to buying multiple managed services, is to host your applications by yourself. Since – this applies to most users at least – you do not take your own hardware, connect to your home Wi-Fi and aim to start your own hosting provider, we need to look at different degrees of self-hosting. Larger organizations, e.g., universities, often like to host applications on their own hardware, within their own network to have full control of their data. Yet, self-hosting exposes you to issues, such as attacks, that you would not need to worry about as much in a software as a service setting (as long as you trust the service).

Self-hosting allows you to host all the applications you want on a dedicated machine. Self-hosters can configure their server depending on their access rights. Offerings range from root access that allows users to do anything to different shades of managed hosting with more moderated access. Backed by virtual infrastructure, modern cloud providers offer a very dynamic form of self-hosting: their clients can use a web GUIs and/or APIs to add, remove, reboot and shut down nodes. Users can spin up anything from pre-configured nodes optimized for different use cases to containerized environments and entire Kubernetes (K8s) clusters in the cloud. Flexible pricing models allow paying based on usage in a very dynamic fashion.

7.3   Building Blocks

Exactly because of this dynamic described above and the ubiquity of the cloud, it is good to know about the building blocks of modern IT infrastructure.

7.3.1   Virtual Machines

Virtual machines (VMs) remain the go-to building blocks for many set-ups. Hence, university IT, private sector IT, independent hosting providers and online giants all offer VMs. Virtual machines allow running a virtual computer that has its own operating system on some host machine. Running applications on such a virtual computer feels like running an application on a standalone computer dedicated to run this application.

> **i**   Oracle's Virtual Box is a great tool to use and try virtual machines locally. Virtual Box allows to run a Virtual Windows or Linux inside macOS and vice versa. Running a virtual box locally may not be the most performant solution, but it allows to have several test environments without altering one's main environment.

7.3.2   Containers and Images

At the first glance, containers look very much like Virtual Machines to the practitioner. The difference is that every Virtual Machine has its own operating system, while containers use the host OS to run a container engine on top of the OS. By doing so, containers can be very lightweight and may take only a few seconds to spin up, while spinning up Virtual Machines can take up to a few minutes – just like booting physical computers. Hence, Docker containers are often used as single-purpose environments: Fire up a container, run a task in that environment, store the results outside the container and shut down the container again.

Docker (Why Docker?[2]) is the most popular containerized solution and quickly became synonymous to container environments configured in a file. So-called Docker images are built layer-by-layer based on other less specific Docker images. A DOCKERFILE is the recipe for a new image. Images are blueprints for containers, an image's running instance. A Docker runtime environment can build images from DOCKERFILEs and distribute these images to an image registry. The platform Docker Hub[3] hosts a plethora of pre-built Docker images from ready-to-go databases to Python ML environments or minimal Linux containers to run a simple shell script in a lab-type environment.

Containers run in a Docker runtime environment and can either be used interactively or in batches which execute a single task in an environment specifically built for this task. One of the reasons why Docker is attractive to researchers is its open character: DOCKERFILEs are a good way to share a configuration in a simple, reproducible file, making it easy to reproduce setups. Less experienced researchers can benefit from Docker Hub which shares images for a plethora of purposes, from mixed data science setups to database configuration. Side effect free working environments for all sorts of tasks can especially be appealing in exotic and/or dependency heavy cases.

Besides simplification of system administration, Docker is known for its ability to work in the cloud. All major cloud hosters offer Docker environments and the ability to deploy Docker containers that were previously developed and tested locally. You can also use Docker to tackle throughput problems using container orchestration tools

---

[2]https://www.docker.com/why-docker
[3]https://dockerhub.com

like Docker Swarm[4] or K8s (say: Kubernetes)[5] to run hundreds of containers (depending on your virtual resources).

7.3.3 Kubernetes

Though hosting Kubernetes (K8s) is clearly beyond the scope of basic level DevOps, the ubiquity of the term and technology as well as the touching points and similarities with the previously introduced concept of containers justify a brief positioning of Kubernetes. We cannot really see Kubernetes as a building block like the technologies introduced above. K8s is a complete cluster with plenty of features to manage the system and its applications. Kubernetes is designed to run on multiple virtual nodes and distribute processes running in so-called pods across its nodes.

Because a plain vanilla Kubernetes cluster is not easy to set up and manage, the tech sector's big three and some of their smaller alternatives offer their own flavors of cloud-based Kubernetes. The basic idea of these offerings is to standardize and to take some of the administrative burden from their clients through pre-configuration and automation support. Red Hat's Openshift is a different approach that targets enterprises who want to set up a cluster on their own infrastructure (on premise).

7.4 Applied Containerization Basics

While the above *Building Blocks* section contextualizes the container approaches, this section gives a simple 101 into the basics of containerization, enabling the readers to take their first steps in the container world. One of the beautiful things about containers is that, due to their isolated nature, one can go a long way trying out things as containers get destroyed and recreated all the time. Also, because containers run in a standardized runtime environment,

---

[4]https://docs.docker.com/engine/swarm/swarm-tutorial/
[5]https://kubernetes.io/

locally developed images easily transfer to large remote machines and clusters.

7.4.1   DOCKERFILEs

*DOCKERFILE*s are text file recipes to create images, i.e., blueprints for containers. One great thing about container images is that they are layered. That is, one can stack images and benefit from previously created images. The below example DOCKERFILE uses a standard, publicly available image from dockerhub.com and adds some custom packages.

```
FROM rocker/shiny:latest
RUN apt-get update
RUN apt-get install -qq -y libpq-dev
RUN install2.r ggplot2 shiny shinydashboard  \
               shinydashboardPlus  \
               dplyr RPostgres
```

In this case, we make use of a pre-built image from the rocker project. The rocker project designs useful images around the R language ecosystem, builds them on a regular basis and makes them available via Docker Hub. Here, our image allows running the open source version of shiny server in a Docker container. We add a Postgres driver at the operating system level before we install several R packages from CRAN.

7.4.2   Building and Running Containers

There are plenty of ways to run and build containers. Online tools either offered as a service or self-hosted can build images server-side. Yet, the easiest way to get started with containers is to run and build them locally with Docker Desktop.

Even though Docker may not even be the best way to build containers to some, Docker is by far the most known way and therefore comes with the largest ecosystem and most community material. Docker Desktop is an easy-to-use application available on Windows and OSX. With Docker Desktop, one can execute Docker

Table 7.1: Basic Docker Commands

Command	Description
docker run	starts application
docker ps	lists containers
docker images	lists docker images
docker pull	pulls images from registry, e.g., dockerhub.com
docker run	runs container based on image
docker kill	kills container
docker build <dir-with-docker-file>	builds image based on DOCKERFILE
docker exec <command> <container>	executes command inside container

commands and build images, either in a GUI or using its CLI. Table 7.1 shows a few of the most basic Docker commands.

To learn what a container looks like, e.g., to find out how the container was affected by changes to the DOCKERFILE, it can be very illustrative to walk around inside. To do so with a container created from the above DOCKERFILE, start the container and execute a bash with the interactive flag -it.

```
docker run -d rocker/shiny
docker exec -it rocker/shiny /bin/bash

# alternative you could start R right away
# note that you need to know the location
# of the executable
docker exec -it rocker/shiny /usr/local/bin/R
```

7.4.3   Docker Compose – Manage Multiple Containers

Docker is a great way to give a new tool a spin without affecting one's proven environment. So, even if you are a container beginner, the time when you would like to spin up multiple containers at once will come quickly. While you can start as many containers as your local resources allow for, running containers at once does not necessarily mean those containers are aware of each other, let alone they could talk to each other.

Modern applications often follow modular architecture patterns, i.e., they have a front end, some middle layer such as a REST API and a database backend. A web application may have a statically generated HTML front and simply expose HTML/CSS/JavaScript files and query a REST API. The REST API may use the express.io framework and is served using a node server which talks to a Postgres database backend. Each of these three parts could live in its own container. This is where docker could help to create a development environment locally that essentially mimics the production setup and therefore facilitates deployment to production.

Docker Compose allows defining how multiple containers play together. Consider the following example file that creates two containers: a Shiny web server and a database which can be queried by the Shiny server.

```
services:
  postgres:
      # a name, e.g.,  db_container is
      # instrumental to be
      # called as host from the shiny app
      container_name: db_container
      build: ./postgres
      restart: always
      environment:
         - POSTGRES_USER=postgres
         - POSTGRES_PASSWORD=postgres
      # This port mapping is only necessary
      # to connect from the host,
      # not to let containers talk to each other.
      ports:
         - "5432:5432"
```

```
        volumes:
            - "./pgdata:/var/lib/postgresql/data"
    shiny:
        container_name: shiny
        depends_on:
            - postgres
        build: ./shiny
        volumes:
            - "./shiny-logs:/var/log/shiny-server"
            - "./shiny-home:/srv/shiny-server"
        ports:
            - "3838:3838"
```

Note how images are built from local directories **postgres** and **shiny** that contain DOCKERFILEs. It is also possible to pull images directly from a registry. To run such a system of multiple containers, simply use

```
docker compose up --force-recreate
```

> **i** Note that *docker-compose* does not replace an orchestrator and cannot provide cluster functionality like Docker Swarm or even Kubernetes.

7.4.4 A Little Docker Debugging Tip

Sometimes containers keep crashing right after they start. This makes debugging a bit harder because we cannot simply use the **-it** flag to get inside and stroll around to find the issue. In such a case, even if you briefly log in, your container will shut down before you can even reach the location in question inside your container. Of course, there are log files

```
docker logs <container-name>
```

Maybe though these logs are not verbose enough, or some permission issue may not be fully covered. Hence, adding 'command: "sleep infinity" to your compose file prevents the service/container in question from running into the problem and crashing immediately.

8

Automation

Make repetitive work fun again!

One aspect that makes a programming approach to data science and analytics appealing is *automation*. Data ingestion, dissemination, reporting or even analysis itself can be repetitive. Particularly shorter update cycles of one's data ask for a way to make yet another iteration pain-free. The following sections look at different forms of automation such as continuous integration and deployment, different forms of workflow automation as well as infrastructure as code.

8.1   Continuous Integration/Continuous Deployment

Because of its origin in build, test and check automation, Continuous Integration/Continuous Deployment (CI/CD)[1] may not be the first thing that comes into mind when one approaches programming through the analytics route. Yet, thorough testing and automated builds have not only become well-established parts of the data science workflow, CI/CD tools can also help to automate tasks beyond testing and packaging your next release.

Modern software providers are an easy way to add the tool chain that is often fuzzily called CI/CD. While CI stands for *continuous integration* and simply refers to a workflow in which the team tries to release new features to production as continuously as possible, CD stands for either *continuous delivery* or *continuous deployment*.

---

[1]See also: https://www.atlassian.com/continuous-delivery/principles/continuous-integration-vs-delivery-vs-deployment

Thanks to infrastructure as code and containerization, automation of development and deployment workflows become much easier also because local development can run in an environment very close to the production setup. Git hosting powerhouses GitHub and GitLab run their flavors of CI/CD tools, making the approach well documented and readily available by default to a wide array of users: GitHub Actions[2] and GitLab CI[3]. In addition, services like CircleCI[4] offer this toolchain independently of hosting git repositories.

Users of the above platforms can upload a simple text file that follows a name convention and structure to trigger a step-based tool-chain based on an event. An example of an event may be a push to a repository's main branch. A common example would be to run tests and/or build a package and upon success deploy the newly created package to some server – all triggered by a simple push to master. One particularly cool thing is, that there are multiple services which allow running the testing on their servers using container technologies. This leads to a great variety of setups for testing. That way, software can easily be tested on different operating systems/environments.

Here is a simple sketch of a *.gitlab-ci.yml* configuration that builds and tests on pushes to all branches and deploys a package after a push to the main branch and successful build and test steps:

```
stages:
- buildncheck
- deploy_pack

test:
image:
name: some.docker.registry.com/some-image:0.2.0
entrypoint:
- ""
```

---

[2]https://docs.github.com/en/actions
[3]https://docs.gitlab.com/ee/ci/
[4]https://circleci.com/

```
stage: buildncheck
artifacts:
untracked: true
script:
# we don't need it and it causes a hidden file NOTE
- rm .gitlab-ci.yml
- install2.r --repos custom.mini.cran.ch .
- R CMD build . --no-build-vignettes --no-manual
- R CMD check --no-manual *.tar.gz

deploy_pack:
only:
- main
stage: deploy_pack
image:
name: byrnedo/alpine-curl
entrypoint: [""]
dependencies:
- 'test'
script:
- do some more steps to login and deploy to server ...
```

For more in depth examples of the above, Jim Hester's talk on GitHub Actions for R[5] is an excellent starting point. CI/CD tool chains are useful for a plethora of actions beyond mere building, testing and deployment of software. The publication chapter covers another common use case: rendering and deployment of static websites. That is, websites that are updated by re-rendering their content at build time, creating static files (artifacts) that are uploaded to web host. Outlets like the GitHub Actions Marketplace, the r-lib collections for R specific actions and the plethora of readily available actions are a great showcase of the broad use of CI/CD applications.

---

[5]https://www.jimhester.com/talk/2020-rsc-github-actions/

8.2 Cron Jobs

Cron syntax is very common in the Unix world and is also useful in the context of the CI/CD tools explained above. Instead of *on dispatch* or *event based* triggers, CI/CD processes can also be triggered based on time.

Named after the Unix job scheduler *cron*, a cron job is a task that runs periodically at fixed times. Pre-installed in most Linux server setups, data analysts often use cronjobs to regularly run batch jobs on remote servers. Cron jobs use a funny syntax to determine when jobs run.

```
#min hour day month weekday
15 5,11 * * 1 Rscript run_me.R
```

The first position denotes the minute mark at which the job runs – in our case 15 minutes after the new hour started. The second mark denotes hours during the day – in our case the 5th and 11th hour. The asterisk * is a wildcard expression for running the job on every day of the month and in every month throughout the year. The last position denotes the weekday, in this example we run our job solely on Mondays.

More advanced expressions can also handle running a job at much shorter intervals, e.g., every 5 minutes.

```
*/5 * * * * Rscript check_status.R
```

To learn and play with more expressions, check crontab guru[6]. If you have more sophisticated use cases, like overseeing a larger number of jobs or execution on different nodes, consider using Apache Airflow[7] as a workflow scheduler.

---

[6]https://crontab.guru/
[7]https://airflow.apache.org/

8.3   Workflow Scheduling: Apache Airflow DAGs

Though much less common than the above tools, Apache Airflow
has earned a mention because of its ability to help researchers
keep an overview of regularly running processes. Examples of such
processes could be daily or monthly data sourcing or timely publication of a regularly published indicator. I often referred to Airflow
as "cronjobs[8] on steroids." Airflow ships with a dashboard to keep
track of many timed processes, plus a ton of other logs and reporting features, which are worth a lot when maintaining reoccurring
processes. Airflow has its own *Airflow Summit* conference, a solid
community and Docker compose setup to get you started quickly.
The setup consists of a container image for the web frontend and
another image for the PostgreSQL backend. The fact that there
is also a *Managed Workflow for Apache Airflow* offering in the
Amazon cloud at the time of writing shows the broad acceptance of
the tool. Airflow also runs on Kubernetes in case you are interested
in hosting Airflow in a more robust production setup.

So, what does Airflow look like in practice? Airflow uses the Python
language to define directed acyclic graphs (DAGs). Essentially, a
DAG pictures a process that has – unlike a cycle – a clear start
and ending. DAGs can be one-dimensional and fully sequential,
but they can also run tasks in parallel.

```
from datetime import datetime, timedelta
from airflow import DAG
# Operators; we need this to operate!
import BashOperator
with DAG(
    default_args={
        "depends_on_past": False,
        "email": ["airflow-admin@your-site.com"],
        "email_on_failure": False,
```

---

[8]https://en.wikipedia.org/wiki/Cron

```
                "email_on_retry": False,
                "retries": 1,
                "retry_delay": timedelta(minutes=5)
            },
            description="Bash Operator"
            schedule='5 11 * * *',
            start_date=datetime(2023, 1, 1),
            catchup=False,
            tags=["example"],
        ) as dag:
            # t1, t2 and t3 are examples of tasks
            # created by instantiating operators
            t1 = BashOperator(
                task_id="print_date",
                bash_command="date > date.txt",
            )

            t2 = BashOperator(
                task_id="sleep",
                depends_on_past=False,
                bash_command="sleep 5",
                retries=3,
            )

            t3 = BashOperator(
                task_id="2 dates",
                depends_on_past=False,
                bash_command="cat date.txt & date",
            )

            t1 >> t2 >> t3
```

The above code shows an example of a simple DAG that combines three strictly sequential tasks. Task *t1* depends on tasks *t2* and *t3*. In this simple example, all tasks use the Airflow *BashOperator* to execute Bash commands, but Airflow provides plenty of other operators from its *PythonOperator*, to *Docker* or *Kubernetes* operators.

Such operators also allow executing tasks on remote machine or clusters, not solely the machine or container that serves Airflow itself.

8.4   Make-Like Workflows

Makefiles and the *make* software that made them popular are the classic of build automation. Best known for its support in the compilation of C programs, Makefiles became popular across programming languages thanks to their straightforward concept and readable approach. A Makefile contains a *target*, an optional prerequisite, and a recipe to get there.

```
target: prerequisite
    recipe
```

Like this:

```
say_yo: store_yo
    cat echo.txt

store_yo:
    echo "yo!" > echo.txt
```

This will simply print

```
echo "yo!" > echo.txt
cat echo.txt
yo!
```

in your terminal. Very much like Apache Airflow and its DAGs which were introduced above, Makefiles allow declaring and managing dependencies. The ability of make and make-like approaches such as the {targets} R package (Landau 2021) goes well beyond the simple sequential definitions like the basic example above. Parallel execution of independent tasks, cherry-picking execution of single tasks from a larger workflow, variables and caching are highly useful when runtime increases. Consider, a multistep workflow, parts of which are running for quite a while but hardly change while other swift parts change all the time, and it becomes obvious how a simple CLI-based workflow helps.

Modern implementation like the target R package ship with network visualizations of the execution path and its dependencies. The walkthrough provided in R OpenSci's book[9] on target is a great summary available as text, code example and video.

8.5   Infrastructure as Code

In recent years, declarative approaches helped to make task automation more inclusive and appealing to a wider audience. Not only a workflow itself, but also the environment a workflow should live and run in is often defined in declarative fashion. This development does not only make maintenance easier, it also helps to make a setting reproducible and shareable.

Do not think infrastructure as code is only relevant for system admins or other infrastructure professionals who make use of it every day. The ability to reproduce and tweak infrastructure at essentially no costs enables other forms of automation such as CI/CD. Just like a flat rate with your mobile carrier will lead to more calls.

infrastructure as code approaches do not only describe infrastructure in declarative and reproducible fashion as stated above; infrastructure-as-code can also be seen as a way to automate setting up the environment you work with. The infrastructure section explains in greater detail how such definitions look like and containers are building blocks of modern infrastructure defined in code.

---

[9]https://books.ropensci.org/targets/walkthrough.html

automation is more complex for cluster setups because among other things, applications need to be robust against pods getting shut down on one node and spawned on another node allowing to host applications in *high availability* mode. On Kubernetes clusters, Helm[10], Kubernetes' package manager, is part of the solution to tackle this added complexity. Helm is, as the Helm website defines "the best way to find share and use software built for Kubernetes". Terraform[11] can manage Kubernetes clusters on clouds like Amazon's AWS, Google's GPC, Microsoft's Azure and many other cloud systems using declarative configuration files. Again, a console-based client interface is used to apply a declarative configuration plan to a particular cloud.

---

[10]https://helm.sh/
[11]https://www.terraform.io/

9

Community

Besides the free-of-license-costs argument, the open source community may be the most popular argument in favor of open source software. And the added value of the community is almost certainly much more valuable than a few green bucks saved on licenses. The support of some of the best communities is so good it may very well outperform an internal IT department specialized elsewhere. Still, developer communities do have their idiosyncrasies. This section intends to help overcome entry barriers and encourage the reader to connect to the developer communities – even if one is not a regular active contributor.

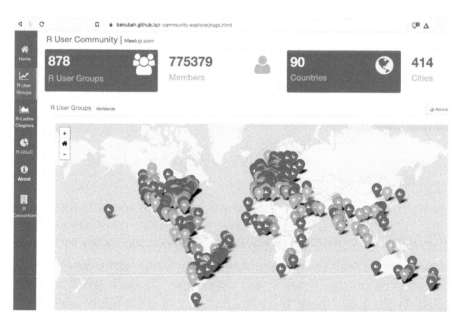

Figure 9.1: R Community Explorer by Ben Ubah. (Source: benubah.github.io/r-community-explorer/rugs.html)

The above figure shows a screenshot of an interactive community explorer tool for the R community. Users can explore user groups and such as R user groups or RLadies chapters around the world. At the time of writing, the tool counted more than 775,000 members of R user groups worldwide and more than 100,000 members of RLadies. The explorer tool and its numbers should not only show you the size of the community, but also help to connect to what has become a very global community.

Apart from user groups of programming languages, the Society of Research Software Engineering[1] is a good way to connect. In addition to the UK-based origin, the society has expanded to other countries and has derivatives in, e.g., the United States[2] or Germany[3]. The main idea of research software engineering societies is to work on a role of software engineering in academia that accounts for the importance and impact of software on modern research. This goes from education in programming to lobbying for acknowledgement of software engineering in academic resumés.

The below sections introduce different channels to connect and interact with the community. Of course, we do not have to use all of these tools and be active in all of these communities, but rather pick some that suit our way of communication.

▬▬▬▬▬▬

9.1   Stay Up-to-Date in a Vastly Evolving Field – Social Media

I hate to admit it because I am not a big fan of social media, but it has definitely become an important channel for professional use also to me. Social media is a great way to get my regular dose of what's new in tech. The popularity of platforms varies locally but also evolves pretty dynamically over time. X, back when it was called Twitter, had been the platform of choice for many engineers

---

[1]https://society-rse.org/
[2]https://us-rse.org/
[3]https://de-rse.org/de/index.html

around data science for almost a decade, before large chunks turned their back on the chirping platform. I am still there[4], but I may have to find a new tool to get feedback and bookmark good reads. No matter the platform, make sure not to get caught in politics, memes or cat pictures if you use it professionally. Because once you strictly limit your time and avoid going down too many rabbit holes, you will get a programming tip here, a nice shortcut there and, more importantly, get a sense of trends and dynamics.

Start with a few accounts to follow, adapt them regularly and use lists in case you need to organize your input a bit more. For *X*, Tweet Deck is a good standard option for a more advanced use of the platform. If you plan to build some following of your own, learn how to schedule posts and put some thought into the timing of your outlet, regarding time zone and audience.

9.2 Knowledge-Sharing Platforms

The most popular knowledge-sharing platform for programmers, stackoverflow.com, has made itself a name for being the first hit in your favorite search engine to any questions or error messages remotely related to source code. The platform has accumulated millions of questions and answers to programming questions across languages. Through a mix of quality content, a community rating system and a healthy mix of gamification, the platform managed to become a mainstay of the programming community. The platform's crowd-based rating system does not only assess the quality of questions and answers, a solid stack Overflow score and reach have also become a notch on programmers' resumés.

---

[4]https://x.com/whatsgoodio

9.3   Look Out for Local Community Group

Speaking of job market opportunities, look out for a local R,
Python} or data science user group. Local user groups around
programming languages do not only host interesting talks or other
formats, they often provide an opportunity to network or even have
dedicated time to advertise open positions. Besides the community
explorer mentioned in the introduction of this chapter, the meetup[5]
platform that has become synonymous with special interest groups
coming together locally, is a good place to start your research.

9.4   Attend Conferences - Online Can Be a Viable Option!

In similar fashion, conferences are a good channel to stay connected
and up-to-date. A conference like PiConf[6], Posit Conf or useR![7] is
basically a bulk meetup: potentially hundreds of talks, thousands
of potential contacts, and quite a bit of time to digest a large
conference. In recent years, conferences often provide an option to
attend online. While, to some, most of the fun and networking will
be missing online, the ability to attend online can also be a great
chance for a conference and its attendance. Online conferences
have the chance to be a lot more inclusive than their in-person
counterparts. Even costs aside, i.e., covered by scholarships, many
cannot afford the time to leave their jobs and families to travel
internationally for an entire week. Online conferences also give
people a chance to attend who may not be involved enough to
attend a software development conference for an entire week, but
who want to catch a glimpse and evaluate. In any case, the entry
hurdle is lower than ever. These paragraphs are meant to convince

---

[5]https://www.meetup.com/
[6]https://piconf.net/
[7]https://x.com/_useRconf

you to take your time, to prepare, attend and debrief a major open source software conference – online or in-person.

9.5   Join a Chat Space

Community chat spaces run by conference organizers, local user groups or societies are another way to stay connected to the community. More dynamic than message boards and forums, chats allow for both asynchronous and live communication. Usually chat spaces are more domain- or even topic-specific than local meetups or social media. Popular software to participate or even run one's own community is Slack[8], Discord[9], Mattermost[10] or Matrix[11]. Slack is available as a service run by a company of the same name. Slack users can start new workspaces for free for hundreds of members, but will have to pay when they want to keep their communities messages beyond the last 10,000 messages. Just like Slack, *Discord* works in our web browsers or as a standalone Desktop or mobile client. Popular among gamers, Discord does not quite have the business attire of Slack, but it certainly has its fans. Mattermost is an open source alternative to the former two. It is also available as a service, but is rather known as a package to self-host one's independent chat space. Matrix has a different approach, labelling itself *an open network for secure, decentralized communication.* Reminiscent of the Internet Relay Chat (IRC)[12] of the old days, Matrix is server software and network of the same name. Just like IRC, Matrix is not bound to a single client and therefore appears modular to the end users allowing to choose between different clients such as Element[13] to connect to established and self-hosted networks alike.

---

[8]https://slack.com
[9]https://discord.com/
[10]https://mattermost.com/
[11]https://matrix.org/
[12]https://en.wikipedia.org/wiki/Internet_Relay_Chat
[13]https://element.io/

10

Publishing and Reporting

Business analysts are used to reporting to management and/or clients regularly. Modern academic research has a similar need for regular updates: Data might get revised or otherwise updated, journals, reviewers and readers will ask for reproducible research. Dissemination of datasets and results in visually appealing as well as machine-readable fashion are important academic, private and public data workers alike.

Because of frequent updates and reproducibility, manually composed outlets become less sustainable. Luckily, Markdown-based reporting offers great solutions for presentations, websites, reports, blogs, office documents or even printed output. Document converters can turn Markdown into HTML/CSS/JavaScript output for flexible use in a standard web browser. Likewise, Markdown renders to PDF or even Microsoft Word.

Approaches such as Quarto[1] (J. J. Allaire et al. 2022), RMarkdown (J. Allaire et al. 2022) or Jupyter Notebooks (Beg et al. 2021) mix plain text with dynamically rendered code chunks that create tables or figures and embed these into the document in the right size and spot. Such a setup is the basis to fully automate the way from analysis to report no matter whether the outlet is printed, a Word document, a presentation, blog or website.

---

[1]https://quarto.org

10.1 Getting Started with a Simple Report

The simplest form of such a Markdown-based output, is a simple HTML report.

To those of us without a web development past or present, HTML may rather sound daunting than simple. But hear me out: HTML is (a) a lot more useful and flexible than newcomers might think and (b) simple indeed: HTML is text, does not need LaTeX to be rendered from Markdown like PDF, and can be displayed by web browsers on a plethora of devices. Plus, based on HTML, you can create (fancy) presentations, websites or simple reports. With the self-contained option, you can even embed included files such as images into one single HTML document using byte encoding. That way, you can easily share a report that can be viewed on any device with a web browser across different operating systems and setups.

To see a Markdown process in action, consider the following basic example of Markdown syntax:

```
#| output: asis


### This is a level three header

This is plain text *this is italic*
and **this is bold**

### This is another level three header

more text
```

When rendered, the above Markdown turns into the below output, stored in HTML and CSS files.

10.1.1   This is a level three header

This is plain text *this is italic* and **this is bold**

10.1.2   This is another level three header

more text

10.2   Static Website Generators

Once we understood how the output files are created, let's take a more in-depth look at how a report goes online in fully automated fashion from computation to a website. In a nutshell, static website generators turn Markdown code into a combination of HTML, CSS and JavaScript, so a web browser can display the result. The Go based Hugo[2] or the classic Jekyll[3] are popular static website generator approaches to run a website or blog.

Approaches such as the {distill} R package (Dervieux et al. 2022) or Quarto, the new kid on the block, add a data science and analytics flavor to the static website generator approach: Those implementations allow running analytics' code at render time. Quarto documents, for example, are text files that contain Markdown text and possibly code chunks in the same documents. When rendered, the analytics code runs first, potentially creating output such as tables or figures. If necessary, this output is stored in separate files and smoothly integrated into the main document that is about to be rendered afterward.

Rendered output often consists of multiple files such as HTML documents, CSS style information, JavaScript code or images. Because this may be fine for websites but inconvenient for presentations or the exchange of reports, analytics-minded renderers such as Quarto offer a **self-contained** option. When enabled, Quarto renders a

---

[2]https://gohugo.io/
[3]https://jekyllrb.com/

single self-contained, encoded HTML file that contains everything from JavaScript to images.

10.3 Hosting Static Websites

Because the requirements of a static website are minimal, we can essentially use the simplest website host possible to host our static site. Unlike with content management system approaches such as WordPress, static websites do not need server side scripting languages or databases. This simplicity allows hosting static websites on a plethora of cheap hosters, including many free plans.

10.3.1 GitHub Pages

One excellent and simple solution to host blogs, personal websites, online documentation or presentations is to use the offerings of major git providers such as GitHub's GitHub Pages[4]. Though originally meant to be used with themes provided by GitHub and Markdown rendered by Jekyll on GitHub's servers, GitHub Pages became the home of an abundance of static sites rendered by a wide array of static website generators.

All you need is a repository on GitHub to host the static files. You can activate GitHub Pages for your repository and choose whether you rather want the rendered files to be on a separate branch named *gh-pages* or in a subfolder of your root directory (mostly docs). Personally, I favor using a separate *gh-pages* branch because git would track every single change made to the automatically rendered content, leading to a messy git history.

By convention, the corresponding static website of a git repository is exposed at `<username>.github.io/<repository-name>`. For GitHub organizations which are popular to group repositories, the exposed URL would be `<orgname>.github.io/<repository-name>`.

---

[4]https://pages.github.com/

> **i** Note
>
> Note that the online version of the book you are currently reading is hosted in very similar fashion: `rse-book.github.io`

10.3.2   GitHub Actions

Hosting a website on a modern git platform comes with an intriguing option: the use of continuous integration tools, as discussed in Chapter 8 on automation. CI/CD is capable of not only rendering Markdown, but can even run computations and virtually any prerequisite step thanks to the underlying docker technology. CI/CD certainly introduces a setup hurdle, but it allows integrating users who do not have the necessary stack installed to execute the render process locally.

10.3.3   Netlify

The Netlify[5] platform does not host git repositories like GitHub or Bitbucket, but it rather focuses on the *build* part. Netlify supports the user in setting up the build process and offers a few add-ons such as Netlify forms to allow for website features that can process user interaction such as online forms. Also, unlike git platforms, Netlify integrates domain purchase into its own platform. Note that Netlify and git are complementary, not mutually exclusive approaches. Platforms like Netlify and GitHub use application programming interfaces (APIs) to communicate with each other, allowing to trigger Netlify builds based on changes to a GitHub repositories.

Basic GitHub Pages setups are good enough for online documentation of most software or other sites that simply display static content. Netlify cannot only improve convenience when using advanced features, but it can also extend possibilities for static websites when needed.

---

[5]https://netlify.app/

10.4 Visualization

Visualization is a powerful tool to communicate insights derived from data analysis. Good visual communication can not only summarize large datasets, but it also can make your report – and therefore your insights – accessible to a wider audience. No matter if you are working on an online outlet or a printed publication of your analysis, it is safe to say that either channel benefits from aesthetically pleasant and concise visualization. Proficiency in data visualization is an indispensable part of a researcher's or analyst's toolbox.

Although plots may look similar across channels, opportunities and challenges plots optimized for online use and traditional printed figures are substantially different. Obviously, the beholder cannot interactively adjust parameters in printed images, while online visualization can be interactive and needs to adapt to varying screens and devices. Hence, the visualization toolbox offers libraries with very different approaches.

10.4.1 Rendered Graphs

The idea of visualization libraries that create rendered graphs is straightforward to understand. Libraries such as R's ggplot2 (Hadley Wickham 2016) or Python's matplotlib (Hunter 2007) fix the dots per inch (dpi) at render time. When writing to disk, such a graph is typically saved as a .png or .jpg file[6]. To the end user, handling such graphs is rather intuitive, as it feels similar to handling photos or screenshots: We have to handle single image files that we can easily preview with onboard tools of all major operating systems. But just like with a photo, if the resolution of an existing image is too small for our next use case, scaling the image up will lead to interpolation, i.e., loss in quality. To see the effect, take a closer look at the two .png files below: The second image

---

[6]When file size is not relevant, .png is usually preferred because it allows for transparent backgrounds.

doubles the width of the first image. Because of interpolation, the text looks blurred, particularly in its curves.

rendered

rendered

A streamlined publication workflow, such as the Quarto-based approach described above, mitigates the problem because this type of workflow automation reduces the effort of resizing, re-rendering and fitting graphs into the current document. Further mitigation comes from extensions packages such as R's gganimate (Pedersen and Robinson 2022) that allows to animate graphs created with ggplot2. Though you might miss out on bleeding-edge interaction and the maximum flexibility of libraries with an online focus, rendered graphs created with a powerful library such as ggplot or matplotlib are a solid way to go for most people's use cases. The likes of ggplot2 have home court advantage in all things printed and still look decent in most online outlets.

10.4.2   JavaScript Visualization Libraries

To those old enough to remember, JavaScript visualization may be reminiscent of a Japanese game convention at night: colorful and blinking. But the visualization knowledge embedded in modern JavaScript libraries and the maximum out-of-the-box opportunities of libraries like Apache echarts (Li et al. 2018), Data Driven Documents (d3js.org) (Bostock, Ogievetsky, and Heer 2011) or Highcharts[7] have very little in common with the JavaScript of the

---

[7]https://www.highcharts.com/

web of the late-90s. In 2022, online communication can take your data visualization to another level.

Today, there are basically two popular JavaScript-based approaches to data visualization: SVG manipulation and HTML5 drawing. No matter whether which one you choose, the opportunities are just off the charts (pun intended): From basic bar charts, scatter plots, candle stick and radar charts to heatmaps, treemaps, 3D and spatial charts, there is hardly anything web based visualization cannot do. And if you really needed special treatment, there is an API to extend your possibilities even. Let us quickly dive into both options.

With the advent of widespread Scalable Vector Graphics (SVG) support in mainstream web browsers about a decade ago, the online ecosystem enabled numerous options to add channel-specific value to visualization. Unlike formats with fixed resolutions like .gif, .jpg or .png formats, vector graphics are not only scalable without loss, but they are also defined inside your HTML document. This opens up the possibility to manipulate them easily using JavaScript as if they were objects of the DOM[8]. Mapping data to SVG aesthetics is the exact idea of the [Data Driven Documents (D3), one of the most popular and powerful visualization libraries. For example, your data may drive the size of dots or any other object, e.g., a car pictogram for when you want to visualize the number of car registrations. The above example shows a strength of the SVG approach: one can use existing SVGs without having to draw them from scratch using JavaScript.

HTML5, on the other hand, is the latest approach and offers more options to support varying screen sizes and device types. While a look into mobile friendliness is beyond the scope of this book, I would like to show an example of how a screen medium (compared to print) can add value. Consider an interactive time series chart of a long-term economic indicator. Depending on the question at hand, you may be interested in the indicator's development over

---

[8]The Document Object Model (DOM) is the hierarchical definition of an HTML website, which in today's web is modified by JavaScript.

decades or rather look at the last couple of years or months. Add a zoom window to not only switch between views, but to also continuously zoom in or out on some crisis or boom or draw an intertemporal comparison between different peaks and lows.

```
library(echarts4r)
library(kofdata)
library(tsbox)


tsl <- get_time_series('ch.kof.barometer')
t_df <- ts_df(tsl$ch.kof.barometer)
t_df |>
    e_charts(time) |>
    e_line(value, symbol = "none") |>
    e_datazoom(type = "slider") |>
    e_title("Demo: Interactivity Adds Value")
```

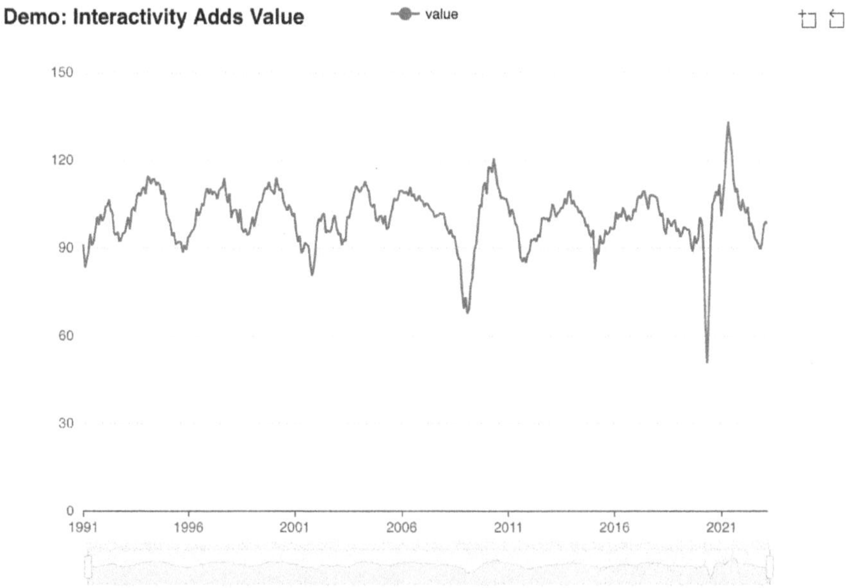

Figure 10.1: Screenshot of an interactive chart created with echarts. Check the online book for the interactive version: https://rse-book.github.io/publishing.html#visualization

Besides more universal libraries like D3 or echarts with all their options and opportunities, there are a few smaller libraries that are much less powerful but a lot simpler to master. Libraries like dygraphs are limited to, e.g., time series but are focused on making that one thing as convenient and inclusive as possible. Depending on your needs, such a smaller library may be an excellent option. Also, when creating a wrapper package, it is obviously easier to implement and maintain only a couple of graphics types as opposed to several hundreds.

10.5   Data Publications

As mentioned in Chapter 6, publishing data on research repositories and catalogs is important not only to make research reproducible, but to help data workers to get credit for their contribution to research. Archives like Zenodo[9] provide GitHub integration to automate data releases and versioning of data. In addition, archives can parse the citation file format (.cff)[10] and generate unique object identification (DOI) numbers for your dataset as well a meta information for the archive entry. Thanks to rOpenSci, there is also curated R package called {cffr} (Hernangómez 2021) to help generate citation files.

---

[9]https://zenodo.org
[10]https://citation-file-format.github.io/

11

Case Studies

While the rest of the book provided more of a big picture type of insight, this section is all about application-minded examples that most of the time feature code to reproduce.

11.1   SSH Key Pair Authentication

This section could be headed "log in like a developer". SSH Key Pairs (often referred to as "RSA key pairs" because of the popular RSA encryption process) are a convenient, relatively secure way to log into an account. SSH-based connections, including secure copy (SCP), often make use of SSH Key Pairs instead of using a combination of username and password. Also, most git platforms use this form of authentication. The basic idea of key pairs is to have a public key and a private key. While the private key is never shared with anyone, the public key is shared with any server you want to log in to. It's like getting a custom door for any house that you are allowed to enter: share your public key with the server admin/web portal, and you'll be allowed in when you show your private key. In case you lose your private key or suspect it has been stolen, simply inform the admin, so they can remove the door (public key). This is where a little detail comes into play: you can password protect the authentication process. Doing so buys you time to remove the key from the server before your password gets brute-forced. The downside of this additional password is its need for interaction. So, when you are setting up a batch that talks to a remote server, that is when you do *not* want a key without a password.

Step one en route to logging in like a grown up, is to create an RSA key pair. GitHub has a [1-2-3 type of manual[1] to get it done. Nevertheless, I would like to show the TL;DR R Studio (Server) specific way here.

1. Login to your Posit Workbench, RStudio Server or start your Desktop RStudio IDE.
2. Go to *Tools → Global Options → Git/SVN*.
3. Hit Create RSA KEY (When you have some crazy ASCII art reminiscent of a rabbit, it's just ok.)
4. Click 'View Public Key'.
5. Copy this key to your clipboard.
6. You can paste the key you obtained to your GitHub settings or put it into your server's authorized keys file.
7. Doing so allows your SSH agent to clone and interact with remote git repositories via SSH or log in to a server if your user is allowed to use a login shell by the server.

11.2 Application Programming Interfaces

An Application Programming Interface (API) is an interface to facilitate machine-to-machine communication. An interface can be anything, any protocol or pre-defined process. But, of course, there are standard and not-so-standard ways to communicate. Plus some matter-of-taste types of decisions. But security and standard compliance are none of the latter. There are standards such as the popular, URL-based REST that make developers' lives a lot easier – regardless of the language they prefer.

Many services such as Google Cloud, Amazon Webservices (AWS), your university library, your favorite social media platform or your local metro operator provide an API. Often, either the platform itself or the community provides what's called an API wrapper: A

---

[1]https://docs.github.com/en/free-pro-team@latest/github/authenticating-to-github/generating-a-new-ssh-key-and-adding-it-to-the-ssh-agent

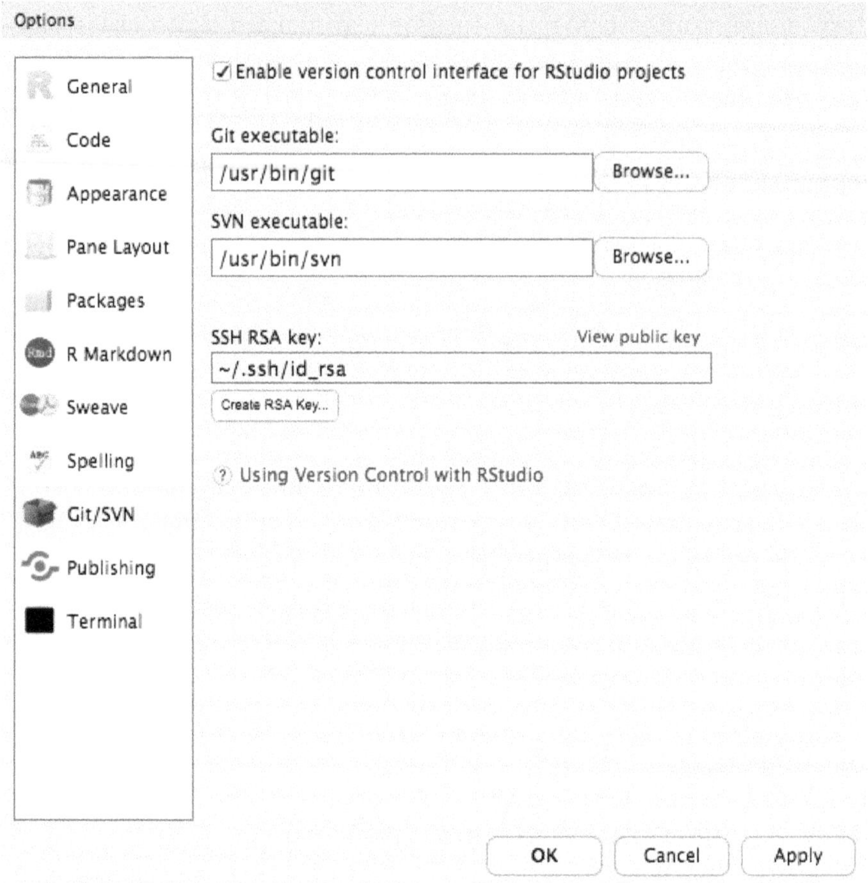

Figure 11.1: The R Studio GUI is an easy way to create a key pair. (Source: screenshot RStudio IDE taken in 2021.)

simple program wraps the process of using the interface through dynamic URLs into a parameterized function. Because the hard work is done server-side by the API backend, building API wrappers is fairly easy, and, if you're lucky, wrappers for your favorite languages exit already. If that is the case, end users can simply use functions like `get_dataset(dataset_id)` to download data programmatically.

```
    URLencode(keyword))
    fromJSON(url)
}
```

You can use these IDs with another endpoint to receive the pictures themselves[3].

```
download_met_images_by_id <-
  function(ids,
           download = "primaryImage",
           path = "met") {
  # Obtain meta description objects from MET API
  obj_list <- lapply(ids, function(x) {
    uri <- "https://collect..."
    req <- download.file(sprintf(uri,
    x),destfile = "temp.json")
    fromJSON("temp.json")
  })


  public <- sapply(obj_list, "[[", "isPublicDomain")


  # Extract the list elements that contains
  # img URLs in order to pass it to the download function
  img_urls <- lapply(obj_list, "[[", download)

  # Note the implicit return, no return statement needed
  # last un-assigned statement is returned
  # from the function
  for (x in unlist(img_urls[public])){
    download.file(x, destfile = sprintf("%s/%s",
      path, basename(x)))
  }
```

---

[3]Full URL used in the below code example: https://collectionapi.
metmuseum.org/public/collection/v1/objects/%d

```
message(
  sprintf("
  The following images ids were not public
  domain and could not be downloaded:\n %s",
          paste(ids[!public], collapse = ",")
))

message(
  sprintf("
  The following images ids were public
  domain and could be downloaded to\n %s: %s",
          path, paste(ids[public], collapse = ",")
))

}
```

Finally, execute the functions: first, search for images with umbrellas, second, download these images by ID. Note that even if I do not display the image itself in the book to err on the side of caution w.r.t. to image property rights, the below code shows availability is checked, and an image is actually downloaded to a previously created folder called *met*.

```
# Step 4: Use the Wrapper
umbrella_ids <- search_met("umbrella")
umbrella_ids$total
```

```
[1] 722
```

```
head(umbrella_ids$objectIDs)
```

```
[1] 491511  19840  19958   9167 122311 121842
```

```
download_met_images_by_id(umbrella_ids$objectIDs[30:33])
```

```
The following images ids were not public
domain and could not be downloaded:
```

```
121919,121922,121809
```

```
The following images ids were public
domain and could be downloaded to
met: 157159
```

```
 dir("met")
```

```
character(0)
```

Wonder what's really in the image? Umbrella or not :)? Try to reproduce this example or come up with your own wrapper from scratch.

11.3   Create Your Own API

The ability to expose data is a go-to skill to make research reproducible and credible. Especially when data get complex and require thorough description in order to remain reproducible for others, a programmatic, machine-readable approach is the way to go.

11.3.1   GitHub to Serve Static Files

Exposing your data through an API is not something for which you would necessarily need a software engineer, let alone your own server infrastructure for. Simply hosting a bunch of .csv spreadsheets alongside a good description (in separate files!!) on, e.g., GitHub for free is an easy and highly available solution.

The swissdata project[4] proposes an implementation of such an approach. The project transforms all sorts of datasets into .csv spreadsheets to contain a cleaned version of the data alongside .json files that contain the data descriptions. The demo[5] describes the implementation in a greater detail and hands on fashion.

---

[4]https://github.com/swissdata
[5]https://github.com/swissdata/demo

If you add a naming convention for your files to such an implementation, you already have a solid interface to a data science environment. Consider the following simple R wrapper that downloads both data and metadata first and then reads both into R[6]. (Alternatively, direct streaming would be possible, too.)

```r
library(jsonlite)
download_swissdata <- function(dataset){
    d_ext <- ".csv"
    m_ext <- ".json"
    d <- sprintf("%s%s", dataset, d_ext)
    m <- sprintf("%s%s", dataset, m_ext)
    gh_url <- "https://raw.git...")
    download.file(file.path(gh_url, d), d)
    download.file(file.path(gh_url, m), m)
}
```

```r
download_swissdata("ch_adecco_sjmi")
```

Now, read the data from disk into your R session

```r
d <- read.csv("ch_adecco_sjmi.csv")
head(d)
```

```
  idx_type        date value
1      sch  2003-03-01  31.9
2     pzua  2003-03-01  12.9
3      ins  2003-03-01   4.9
4      unw  2003-03-01  14.2
5      sch  2004-03-01  36.4
6     pzua  2004-03-01  12.2
```

As well as the nested meta information{nested data}. JSON maps 1:1 to R lists. Hence, both the on-disk representation and the

---

[6]Full URL of the below code example: https://raw.githubusercontent. com/swissdata/demo/master/data

in-memory representation are equally well suited for nested data. The below example shows a sub-label element containing description in multiple languages.

```
m <- fromJSON("ch_adecco_sjmi.json")
m$labels$idx_type$unw
```

```
$en
[1] "Company websites"

$de
[1] "Unternehmens-Webseiten"

$fr
named list()

$it
named list()
```

> **i** Note
>
> Note, standard GitHub repositories are not well suited to host larger files or binaries. Check out their file hosting offering or consider other services focused on files.

11.3.2 Simple Dynamic APIs

Even, going past serving static files, does not require much software development expertise. Thanks to frameworks such as express.js or the {plumbr} package in the R ecosystem, it is easy to create an API that turns an URL into a parameterized server-side action. Before we look at one of those frameworks in greater detail, let's take a look at the two most common HTTP request methods[7] GET and POST.

---

[7] https://developer.mozilla.org/en-US/docs/Web/HTTP/Methods

According to Mozilla's definition, the GET method "requests a representation of the specified resource. Requests using GET should only retrieve data," while POST "submits an entity to the specified resource, often causing a change in state or side effects on the server". Obviously, there are many other methods for the HTTP protocol, but the above two should help to understand the idea behind standard compliant REST web application programming interfaces.

Let's assume you have a working nodejs[8] JavaScript runtime environment installed on your local development machine, so you can run JavaScript files outside a web browser. Such a setup mimics the situation on a web server with Node.js installed. Also, let's assume you have npm[9] installed as a package manager to facilitate installing node packages from the npm open source package registry.

First, create a folder `api`, go to the freshly created directory and initiate a node package.

```
# run initialization in a dedicated folder
mkdir api
cd api
mkdir public
npm init
```

Just sleepwalk through the interactive dialog accepting all defaults. This created a package.json file to keep track of dependencies and their package versions used in your project. Once done, add express using the npm package manager.

```
npm install express
```

Now, that we installed the JavaScript framework Express.js, we can use the framework to create a minimal web application that serves an API endpoint using the node runtime environment. Consider a minimal hello-world example that does about the same as the static file example of the previous action:

---

[8]https://nodejs.org/en/
[9]https://npmjs.com

```
const express = require('express')
const app = express()
const port = 3000

app.get('/', (req, res) => {
  res.send('Hello World!')
})

app.use('/static', express.static('public'))


app.listen(port, () => {
  console.log(`RSE demo app listening on port ${port}`)
})
```

The first `app.get` route simply maps the root, a plain, un-nested starting point so to say, in our case `localhost:3000/` to the output of the `res.send` call. The second `app` command serves the content of the `public` folder to visitor's of `localhost:3000/static`. So if a `public/` folder inside the app folder contained a cover image of my *Hacking for Science* courses, this would be served at `localhost:3000/static/h4sci.jpeg`.

Now let us make use of server-side features beyond simply serving static files and add the need for an API key to get the picture.

```
const express = require('express')
const app = express()
const port = 3000

app.get('/', (req, res) => {
  res.send('Hello World!')
})

app.use('/static', (req, res, next) => {
  var key = req.query['api_key'];
  if (!key) res.send('api key required');
  if (apiKeys.indexOf(key) === -1)  res.send('eh-eh,
```

Figure 11.2: Cover illustration of the Hacking for Science Courses.
(Source: own illustration.)

```
    wrong key.');
  req.key = key;
  next();
})



// NOTE THAT this is only a
// demo example (!)
// DO NOT use insecure passwords
// in production.
// Make sure to find better ways
// to secure your keys!
// also transferring keys in URLs
// via GET is not optimal,
// consider using an upfront
// authentication method
var apiKeys = ['abc','123'];
```

```
app.use('/static', express.static('public'))

app.listen(port, () => {
  console.log(`RSE demo api listening on port ${port}`)
})
```

We simply added a mount point using `app.use` (instead of `app.get`) which makes sure that everything past `/static` is affected by the logic added to this mount. So, our `Hello World!` greeting is out there for anybody to see, while displaying the picture whose URL starts with `/static` needs an API key. Though this is only one, admittedly made up example of mapping URLs and parameters to functions via HTTP(S), it hints at the possibilities of dynamic APIs from database queries to web forms and many other applications. The above example shows also how frameworks like Express JavaScript[10] or plumber (Schloerke and Allen 2022) facilitate the definition of machine-to-machine interfaces even for less experienced developers. The impact of frameworks is not limited to the technical implementation, though. Developers benefit from comprehensive approaches like Swagger and the OpenAPI specification during the conceptual part of creating machine to machine interfaces.

11.4   A Minimal Webscraper: Extracting Publication Dates

Even though KOF Swiss Economic Institute offers a REST API to consume publicly available data, publication dates are unfortunately not available through in API just yet. Hence, to automate data consumption based on varying publication dates, we need to extract upcoming publication dates of the Barometer from KOF's media release calendar. Fortunately, all future releases are presented online in an easy-to-scrape table. So, here's the plan:

---

[10]https://expressjs.com/

1. Use Google Chrome's *inspect element* developer feature to find the X-Path (location in the Document Object Model) of the table.

2. Read the web page into R using `rvest`.

3. Copy the X-Path string to R to turn the table into a data.frame

4. Use a regular expression to filter the description for what we need.

First, let's take a look at our starting point, the media releases sub-page, first.

Figure 11.3: The KOF Swiss Economic Institute's media agenda in 2021. (Source: screenshot Google Chrome browser.)

The website looks fairly simple, and the jackpot is not hard, presented in a table right in front of us. Can't you smell the data.frame already?

Right-click the table to see a Chrome context window pop up. Select *inspect*.

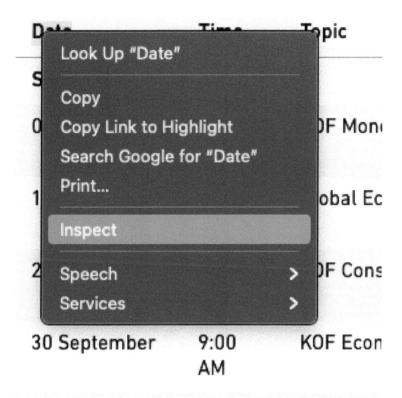

Figure 11.4: Modern browsers come with developer tools built in to help you expect a website's source code. (Source: screenshot Google Chrome browser.)

Hover over the highlighted line in the source code at the bottom. Make sure the selected line marks the table. Right click again, select copy → copy X-Path[11].

---

[11]Full URL used in the below code example: https://kof.ethz.ch/news-und-veranstaltungen/medien/medienagenda.html

Figure 11.5: Browser tools help you explore the hierarchical structure of a website in interactive fashion. (Source: screenshot Google Chrome browser.)

On to R!

```r
library(rvest)
# URL of the media release subsite
url <- "https://kof.ethz.ch..."
# Extract the DOM object from the path we've
# previously detected using
# Chrome's inspect feature
table_list <- url %>%
  read_html() %>%
  html_nodes(xpath = '
  //html/body/div[6]/section/div/section
  /div[2]/div/div[3]/div/div/div/
  div/div/div/div/table') %>%
  # turn the HTML table into an R data.frame
  html_table()
# because the above result may potentially contain
# multiple tables, we just use
# the first table. We know from visual
# inspection of the site that this is the
# right table.
agenda_table <- table_list[[1]]

# *[@id="t-6b2da0b4-cec0-47a4-bf9d-
#   bbfa5338fec8-tbody-row-2-cell-2"]

# extract KOF barometer lines
pub_date <- agenda_table[grep("barometer",
                         agenda_table$X3),]
pub_date
```

Yay! We got everything we wanted. Ready to process.

11.5 Automate Script Execution: An Example with GitHub Actions

containerization as described in the infrastructure section has standardized virtual hardware into building blocks that are available across different platforms and providers. This development has led to a wide array of offerings that allow us to run our code in a language-agnostic environment. In addition to the major cloud platforms, git providers that offer a CI/CD tool chain are a good option to run our code on a remote container. Though originally designed mostly for build automation, CI/CD such as GitHub actions can be used to automate a variety of tasks by running them on a container. Consider the following minimal R script that we will run on GitHub actions.

```
#!/usr/bin/env Rscript

library(knitr)
knit("README.Rmd")
```

The script uses {knitr} to render an RMarkdown document to a Markdown document that is automatically rendered to a pretty HTML file when pushed to a repository hosted on GitHub.

> **i Note**
>
> Notice the common *shebang* comment that defines the executable for batch execution of a script file – in this case *Rscript* to run R outside of an interactive R session.

Embedded in a bit of descriptive text before and after the code, the main code chunk of the .Rmd template file is equally straightforward:

```
library(kofdata)
library(tsbox)
tsl <- get_time_series("ch.kof.barometer")
ts_plot(tsl$ch.kof.barometer)
cat(sprintf("last update on %s.",
 as.character(Sys.Date())))
```

We make use of the {kofdata} API wrapper to obtain data from the KOF Data API and use the {tsbox} to visualize the time series data we received. Finally, we print the system date of the runtime environment – in our case the GitHub Actions Docker container. Running the README.**Rmd** file yields two artifacts: (1) a README.**md** file and a (2) .png graph located in a `figure/` folder. Because the above runs inside a temporary single purpose container, our workflow needs to make sure those artifacts are stored persistently.

The below .yaml file defines the environment and workflow for GitHub Actions. When located properly according to GitHub's convention, i.e., in a hidden `github/worflows` folder, GitHub identifies the .yaml file as input and allows executing the workflow. (Standalone build tools like Woodpecker or other integrated CI/CD tools like GitLab CI/CD use very similar workflow definitions).

```
# Simple data transformation workflow
name: KOF Economic Barometer

# Controls when the action will run.
# Triggers the workflow on push or pull request
# events but only for the main branch
on:
  workflow_dispatch

jobs:
  kof:
    runs-on: ubuntu-latest
```

```
    container: rocker/verse
    steps:
      - uses: actions/checkout@v3
      - run: git version
      - run: rm -rf README.md
      - run: |
          Rscript -e \
          && 'install.packages(c("kofdata","tsbox"))'
          chmod +x demo_gha.R
          ./demo_gha.R
      - run: ls -lah
      - run: |
          git config --global --add safe.directory \
          && /__w/h4sci-gha-demo/h4sci-gha-demo
          git config --global user.name \
          && "Matt Bannert"
          git config --global user.email \
          && "mbannert@users.noreply.github.com"
          git add figure README.md
          git commit -m \
          && "Update README.md via GH Actions"
          git push
```

First, the below file gives our workflow a name to identify the workflow among other workflows defined within the same repository. The **on** block defines what triggers the workflow. The **workflow_dispatch** option is a rather uncommon trigger, as it simply means the workflow can be triggered by pressing a button in GitHub's Web GUI. Cronjob-based triggers or triggers based on git actions such as pushes to a certain branch are more common as we are looking to avoid interaction at runtime. Inside the job definitions itself, we first define the operating system of the host and the Docker image in which our process should run.

Then, walk through the single steps of our workflow. Notice that **actions/checkout@v3** is different from the other steps because it is taken from GitHub's marketplace for actions. Instead of writing standard operations, namely checking out the git repository we're working with to the container that runs the action, from scratch, we use the marketplace action for that. Be aware though that there is a trade-off between convenience and transparency. When I was teaching this year and wanted to recycle an example from the previous year, it was not all that convenient. Only one year later, my example that leaned heavily on marketplace actions was not working anymore. What's worse is that it was also relatively hard to debug because I had to deal with the inner workings of a dependency heavy implementation that I would not have implemented this way. If we look at the above steps after the checkout action, we see a list of simple steps that are easy to read: first, simply print the git version to make sure git is working inside the container, and we know its version in case we need to debug. Second, we remove the README.md file we have just checked out. This file will be replaced anyway, and we want to avoid any rights conflicts overwriting the file. Then we run R in batch to install two more specific packages to the R environment running inside the container. Because we use a pre-built *tidyverse* images from the rocker project, we do not have to install R itself and many common packages. We continue to use the *chmod* Linux command to change the access rights of our minimal R script. With the *shebang* comment inside the file, we can directly execute the .R file with the ./ prefix because it knows which executable to use to run it. Finally, we take a look at the content of the current folder before we commit and push all the files we generated back to our GitHub repository. After the process is done, the container will stop and removed.

---

i Note

Note that we can see all the output of the process from the GitHub actions menu on our repository's website. This is why it's useful to print outputs of intermediate steps.

11.6   Choropleth Map: Link Data to a GeoJSON Map File

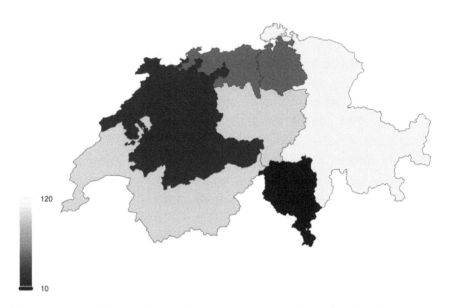

Figure 11.6: Screenshot of an interactive choropleth; for the actual, interactive visualization visit https://rse-book.github.io/case-studies.html#sec-map

Data visualization is a big reason for researchers and data analysts to look into programming languages. Programming languages do not only provide unparalleled flexibility, but they also make data visualization reproducible and allow placing charts in different contexts, e.g., websites, printed outlets or social media.

One of the more popular types of plots that can be created smoothly using a programming language is the so-called *choropleth*. A *choropleth* maps values of a variable that is available by region to a given continuous color palette on a map. Let's break down the ingredients of the below map of Switzerland[12].

First, we need a *definition of a country's shape*. Those definitions come in various formats, from traditional *shape files* to web-friendly *GeoJSON*. Edzer Pebesma's useR! 2021 keynote[13] has a more thorough insight.

Second, we need some data.frame that simply connects values to regions. In this case, we use regions defined by the Swiss Federal Statistical Office (FSO). Because our charting library makes use of the GeoJSON convention to call the region label "name" we need to call the column that holds the region names "name" as well. That way, we can safely use defaults when plotting. Ah, and note that the values are absolutely bogus that came to my mind while writing this (so please do not mull over how these values were picked).

```
d <- data.frame(
   name = c("Zürich",
            "Ticino",
            "Zentralschweiz",
            "Nordwestschweiz",
            "Espace Mittelland",
            "Région lémanique",
            "Ostschweiz"),
   values = c(50,10,100,50,23,100,120)
)
```

Finally, we are calling our charting function from the *echarts4r* package. {echarts4r} (Li et al. 2018) is an R wrapper for the feature-rich Apache Echarts JavaScript plotting library. The example uses the base R pipes (available from 4+ on, former versions needed to use pipes via extension packages.). Pipes take the result of one previous line and feed it as input into the next line. So, the

---

[12]Full URL used in the below example https://raw.githubusercontent.com/mbannert/maps/master/ch_bfs_regions.geojson

[13]https://www.youtube.com/watch?v=cK08bxUJn5A

data.frame *d* is linked to a charts instance and the *name* column is used as the link. Then a map is registered as *CH* and previously read JSON content is used to describe the shape.

```
d |>
  e_charts(name) |>
  e_map_register("CH", json_ch) |>
  e_map(serie = values, map = "CH") |>
  e_visual_map(values,
                  inRange = list(color = viridis(3)))
```

Also note the use of the viridis functions which returns three values from the famous, colorblind friendly viridis color palette.

```
viridis(3)
```

```
[1] "#440154FF" "#21908CFF" "#FDE725FF"
```

Here's the full example:

```
library(echarts4r)
library(viridisLite)
library(jsonlite)

json_ch <- jsonlite::read_json(
  "https://raw.github..."
)



d <- data.frame(
  name = c("Zürich",
           "Ticino",
           "Zentralschweiz",
           "Nordwestschweiz",
           "Espace Mittelland",
           "Région lémanique",
```

```
               "Ostschweiz"),
    values = c(50,10,100,50,23,100,120)
  )

  d |>
    e_charts(name) |>
    e_map_register("CH", json_ch) |>
    e_map(serie = values, map = "CH") |>
    e_visual_map(values,
                    inRange = list(color = viridis(3)))
```

11.7 Web Applications with R Shiny

To start, let me demystify the {shiny} R package (Chang et al. 2022). There are basically two reasons why so many inside data science and analytics have Shiny on their bucket list of things to learn. First, it gives researchers and analysts home court advantage on a web server. Second, it gives our online appearances a kick start in the dressing room.

Don't be surprised though if your web development professional friend outside data science and analytics never heard of it. Compared to web frontend framework juggernauts such as *react, angular* or *vue.js* the Shiny web application framework for R is rather a niche ecosystem.

Inside the data science and analytics communities, fancy dashboards and the promise of an easy, low hurdle way to create nifty interactive visualizations have made {shiny} app development a sought-after skill. Thanks to pioneers, developers and teachers like Dean Attali, John Coene, David Granjon, Colin Fay and Hadley Wickham, the sky seems the limit for R Shiny applications nowadays.

This case study does not intend to rewrite {shiny}'s great documentation or blogs and books around it. I'd rather intend to help you get your first app running asap and explain a few basics along the way.

11.7.1 The Web Frontend

Figure 11.7: Maybe I am late, but I look goood. Johnny representing the frontend. (Source: own illustration.)

Stats and figures put together by academic researchers or business analysts are not used to spending a lot of time in front of the mirror. (Often, for the same reason as their creators: perceived opportunity costs.)

Shiny bundles years worth of limelight experience and online cat-walk professionalism into an R package. Doing so allows us to use all this design expertise through an R interface, abstracting away the need to dig deep into web programming and frontend design (you know the HTML/CSS/JavaScript).

Let's consider the following web frontend put together with a few lines of R code. Consider the following, simple web fronted that lives in a dedicated user interface R file, called *ui.R*:

```r
library(shiny)
library(shinydashboard)

dashboardPage(
  dashboardHeader(title = "Empty App"),
  dashboardSidebar(),
  dashboardBody(
    fluidPage(
      fluidRow(
        box(title = "Configuration",
            sliderInput("nobs",
                        "Number of Observations",
                        min = 100,
                        max = 10000,
                        value = 500),
            sliderInput("mean_in","Mean",
                        min = 0,
                        max = 10,
                        value = 0),
            sliderInput("sd_in","SD",
                        min = 1,
                        max = 5,
                        value = 1),
            width = 4),
        box(title = "Distribution",
            plotOutput("dist"),
            width = 8)
```

```
      ),
      fluidRow(
        box("Tabelle",
            dataTableOutput("tab"),
            width=12
            )
          )
        )
      )
    )
```

Besides the {shiny} package itself, the ecosystem around Shiny brings popular frontend frameworks from the world outside data science to R. In the above case, a boilerplate library for dashboards is made available through the add-on package {shinydashboard} (Chang and Borges Ribeiro 2021).

Take a moment to consider what we get readily available at our fingertips: Pleasant user experience (UX) comes from many things. Fonts, readability, the ability to adapt to different screens and devices (responsiveness), a clean, intuitive design and many other aspects. The {shinydashboard} package adds components like *fluidPages* or *fluidRow* to implement a responsive (Google me!), grid-based design using R. Note also how similar the hierarchical, nested structure of the above code is to HTML tagging. (Here's some unrelated minimal HTML)

```
<!-- < > denotes an opening,
 </ > denotes an end tag. -->
<html>
  <body>
  <!-- anything in between tags is affected by
       the tags formatting.
       In this case bold -->
    <b> some bold title </b>
    <p>some text</p>
```

```
    </body>
  </html>
```

{shiny} ships with many widgets[14] such as input sliders or table outputs that can simply be placed somewhere on your site. Again, add-on packages provide more widgets and components beyond those that ship with Shiny.

11.7.2 Backend

While the frontend is mostly busy looking good, the backend has to do all the hard work, the computing, the querying – whatever is processed in the background based on user input.

Under-the-hood-work that is traditionally implemented in languages like Java, Python or PHP[15] can now be done in R. This is not only convenient for the R developer who does not need to learn Java, it's also incredibly comfy if you got data work to do. Or put differently: who would like to implement logistic regression, random forests or principal component analysis in PHP?

Consider the following minimal backend *server.R* file which corresponds to the above *ui.R* frontend file. The anonymous (nameless) function which is passed on to the *ShinyServer* function takes two named lists, *input* and *output*, as arguments. The named elements of the input list correspond to the *widgetId* parameter of the UI element. In the below example, our well-known base R function *rnorm* takes *nobs* from the input as its *n* sample size argument. Mean and standard deviation are set in the same fashion using the user interface (UI) inputs.

---

[14]online widget galleries like R Studio's shiny widget gallery: https://shiny.rstudio.com/gallery/widget-gallery.html that help to "shop" for the right widgets.

[15]Yes, one could lists JavaScript here, too, but let's keep things simple and think of JavaScript as traditionally client-side here.

Figure 11.8: While the frontend is busy looking spiffy, the backend does the computation work. (Source: own illustration.)

```
library(shiny)

shinyServer(function(input,output){

  output$dist <- renderPlot({
    hist(
      rnorm(input$nobs,
            mean = input$mean_in,
            sd = input$sd_in),
      main = "",
      xlab = ""
      )
  })
```

```
  output$tab <- renderDataTable({
    mtcars
  })
})
```

The vector that is returned from *rnorm* is passed on to the base
R *hist* which returns a histogram plot. This plot is then rendered
and stored into an element of the *output* list. The *dist* name is
arbitrary, but again it matched to the UI. The *plotOutput* function
of *ui.R* puts the rendered plot onto the canvas, so it's on display
in people's browsers. *renderDataTable* does so in analog fashion to
render and display the data table.

11.7.3   Put Things Together and Run Your App

The basic app shown above consists of an *ui.R* and a *server.R* file
living in the same folder. The most straightforward way to run such
an app is to call the *runApp()* function and provide the location of
the folder that contains both of the aforementioned files.

```
library(shiny)
runApp("folder/that/holds/ui_n_server")
```

This will use your machine's built-in web server and run Shiny
locally on your notebook or desktop computer. Even if you never
put your app on a web server and run a website with it, it is
already a legitimate way to distribute your app. If it was part of
an R package, everyone who downloads your package could use it
locally, maybe as a visual inspection tool or a way to derive inputs
interactively and feed them into your R calculation.

11.7.4   Serve Your App

Truth be told, the full hype and excitement of a Shiny app only
comes into play when you publish your app and make it available
to anyone with a browser, not just the R people. Though hosting
is a challenge in itself, let me provide you a quick Shiny specific
discussion here. The most popular options to host a Shiny app are

- **Software-as-a-service (SaaS).** No maintenance, hassle-free, but least bang for the buck. The fastest way to hit the ground running is R Studio's service *shinyapps.io*.

- **On premise, aka in-house.** Either download the open source version of Shiny server, the alternative Shiny proxy or the Posit Connect premium solution and install them on your own Virtual Machine.

- Use a **Shiny server Docker image** and run a container in your preferred environment.

11.7.5   Shiny Resources

One of the cool things of learning shiny is how Shiny, and its ecosystem, allow you to learn quickly. Here are some of my favorite resources to hone your Shiny skills.

Figure 11.9: The {shinydashboard} R package provides customizable skeletons for dashboards. (Source: screenshot of a blank dashboard created with shinydashboard.)

- R Studio Shiny's Widget Gallery: https://shiny.rstudio.com/gallery/widget-gallery.html

- shinydashboard (Chang and Borges Ribeiro 2021): https://rstudio.github.io/shinydashboard

- Mastering Shiny (Hadley Wickham 2021): (https://mastering-shiny.org/)

- Engineering Production Grade Shiny Apps (Fay et al. 2021): https://engineering-shiny.org/

- RInterface by David Granjon, John Coene, Victor Perrier and Isabelle Rudolf: https://rinterface.com/

11.8 Project Management Basics

The art of stress-free productivity, as I once called it in 2010 blog post, has put a number of gurus on the map and a whole strand of literature on our bookshelves. So, rather than adding to that, I would like to extract a healthy, best-of-breed type of dose here. The following few paragraphs do not intend to be comprehensive, not even for the scope of software projects, but inspirational.

In the software development startup community, the *waterfall* approach became synonymous to conservative, traditional and ancient: Over specification in advance of the project, premature optimization and a lawsuit over expectations that weren't met. Though, waterfall projects may be better than their reputation, specifications should not be too detailed and rigid.

Many software projects are rather organized in *agile* fashion, with SCRUM and KANBAN being the most popular derivatives. Because empirical academic projects have a lot in common with software projects inasmuch that there is a certain expectation and quality control, but the outcome is not known in advance. Essentially, in agile project management you roughly define an outcome similar to a minimum viable product (MVP). That way, you do not end up with nothing after a year of back and forth. During the implementation you'd meet regularly, let's say every 10 days, to discuss development since the last meet and the short-term plans for the steps ahead. The team splits work into tasks on the issue tracker and assigns them. Solutions to problems will only be sketched out and discussed bilaterally or in small groups. By defining the work package for only a short timespan, the team stays flexible. In professional setups, agile development is often strictly implemented and makes use of sophisticated systems of roles that developers and project managers can get certified for.

Major git platforms ship with a decent, carpentry-level project management GUI. The issue tracker is at the core of this. If you use it the minimal way, it's simply a colorful to-do list. Yet, with a bit of inspiration and the use of tags, comments and projects, an issue tracker can be a lot more.

☐ ⓘ **5 Open** ✓ 0 Closed

☐ ⓘ **Task 5: Create a Program to Assign Students to Groups** task
     #5 opened 2 days ago by mbannert

☐ ⓘ **Task 4: Descriptive Analysis of the Survey** task
     #4 opened 2 days ago by mbannert

☐ ⓘ **Task 3: Merge Conflict Drill** task
     #3 opened 2 days ago by mbannert   ▤ 0 of 2

☐ ⓘ **Task 2: First Collaborative Git Steps** task
     #2 opened 2 days ago by mbannert   ▤ 0 of 6

☐ ⓘ **Task 1: Get Familiar with Git (local repository functions)** task
     #1 opened 2 days ago by mbannert   ▤ 0 of 4

The GitHub issue tracker (example from one of the course's repositories) can be a lot more than a to-do list.

Swim lanes (reminiscent of a bird's-eye view of an Olympic pool) can be thought of columns that you have to walk through from left to right: To Do, Doing, Under Review, done. (you can also customize the number and label of lanes and event associate actions with them, but let's stick to those basic lanes in this section.) The idea is to use to keep track of the process and make the process transparent.

Figure 11.10: GitHub's web platform offers swim lanes to keep a better overview of issues being worked on. (Source: own GitHub repository.)

> 💡 Tip
>
> No lane except "Done" should contain more than 5–6 issues. Doing so prevents clogging the lanes at a particular stage which could potentially lead to negligent behavior, e.g., careless reviews.

11.9 Parallel Computation

The idea of having multiple workers at your disposal to fix your math problem even quicker than one smart worker seems equally appealing to third graders and researchers. Very much like in school, the ability to assess whether getting help in the first place is worth the overhead and what type of help to get, is the most important skill. The classical challenge where parallel computation using multiple cores really helps is throughput problems, i.e., problems where your tasks are independent of each other. Yet, it may not be clear up-front if the number and computation time of your single tasks justifies the overhead of letting your program know it should split computations across cores and manage memory accordingly. Also, consider that processes can be turned parallel at different levels: you could simply use your local machine's cores and a parallelization implementation such as R's {future} (Bengtsson 2021) or {parallel} packages to parrallelize locally. Or you could go parallel at a machine or container level. While the former is easier as it requires less infrastructure knowledge, it is limited by the resources of your local machine. Of course, if you have access to a HPC cluster, this may not be a disadvantage at all (depending on how your cluster balances load and manages access to resources). In any case, you should make a clear decision at which level you go parallel and avoid nested parallelization.

Let's consider the following example of a simple local parallelization, including a performance benchmark. The following R example uses the {microbenchmark} R package (Mersmann 2021) to check the effect of parallel computing on running seasonal adjustment of multiple time series. Before we start with the actual example, let's create some demo data: We simply create a list with 1000 elements, each of which is the same monthly time series about airline passengers from 1949 to 1960.

```r
data("AirPassengers")
tsl <- list()
for(i in 1:1000){
  tsl[[i]] <- AirPassengers
}
```

Now, let's load the {seasonal} R package (Sax and Eddelbuettel 2018) and perform a basic seasonal adjustment of each of these time series. The first statement performs 100 adjustments sequentially; the second statement uses parallel computing to spread computations across the processors of the machine that ran this example.

```r
library(seasonal)
library(parallel)
library(microbenchmark)
```

```
no_parallel <- function(li, s){
  lapply(li[s],seas)
}

with_parallel <- function(li, s){
  out <- list()
  cl <- makeCluster(detectCores())
  # load 'seasonal' for each node
  clusterEvalQ(cl, library(seasonal))
  parLapply(cl, li[s], function(e) try(seas(e)))
  stopCluster(cl)
}


out <- microbenchmark(
    noparallel10 = no_parallel(tsl, 1:10),
    withparallel10 = with_parallel(tsl, 1:10),
    noparallel100 = no_parallel(tsl, 1:100),
    withparallel100 = with_parallel(tsl, 1:100),
    times = 5,
    unit = "seconds"
)

d <- summary(out)
```

Obviously, the absolute computation time depends on the hardware used as well as the operating system, depending on the task at hand.

As expected, given the perfect independence of the tasks from each other, performance gains are quite substantial (~5.5 times faster) for the above example, though not perfect (on my 8-core machine). Advanced parallel implementations and deeper dives into the way different processors work may further optimize efficiency here.

Table 11.1: Runtimes with and without Parallelization.

(a)

expr	min	lq	mean
noparallel10	2.0390981	2.0445802	2.0549512
withparallel10	0.7002317	0.7223823	0.7511417
noparallel100	20.2986816	20.3512413	20.6002367
withparallel100	3.7620145	3.9777512	4.1239902

(b)

expr	median	uq	max
noparallel10	2.0465370	2.0508339	2.093707
withparallel10	0.7295064	0.7667813	0.836807
noparallel100	20.3891324	20.8755458	21.086582
withparallel100	4.1303562	4.3523015	4.397527

```
library(kableExtra)
kable(d[,c(1:4)],"latex",
      booktabs = TRUE,
      escape= FALSE) |>
      kable_styling(
         latex_options = c("repeat_header")
         ) |>
      column_spec(1:2, width = "2.5cm")
kable(d[,c(1,5,6,7)],"latex",
      booktabs = TRUE,
      escape= FALSE) |>
      kable_styling(
         latex_options = c("repeat_header")
         ) |>
      column_spec(1:2, width = "2.5cm")
```

Yet, the key takeaway from the above exercise is not the parallel computation itself, but the ability to evaluate the need to go parallel and how. Benchmarking does not only help to get a ballpark estimate of the costs should you go outside for more computational power, it gives you an idea whether the gains from a parallel approach are worth the hassle. In other words, of course a computation running four to five times faster than before sounds spectacular, but what if the total runtime is less than a few minutes either way? Development time, particularly for newcomers, is very likely longer than a few minutes. Plus, going parallel jeopardizes your cross-platform compatibility depending on the parallel implementation you use.

Another good use of benchmarking is to run a few smaller case experiments to get an idea of how performance gains evolves when we throw more work at our system. Unlike the below example, performance gains do not necessarily have to be linear. Visualization can give us a better idea.

```
library(ggplot2)
library(viridis)
vizframe <- d[,c(1,5)]
vizframe$iterations <- as.character(c(10,10,100,100))
vizframe$parallel <- c("no","yes","no","yes")
names(vizframe)[2] <- "seconds"

gg <- ggplot(
  vizframe[,-1],
 aes(fill = parallel,
     y = seconds,
     x = iterations))
gg +
  geom_bar(position = "dodge",
           stat = "identity") +
  coord_flip() +
  scale_fill_viridis(discrete = T) +
  theme_minimal()
```

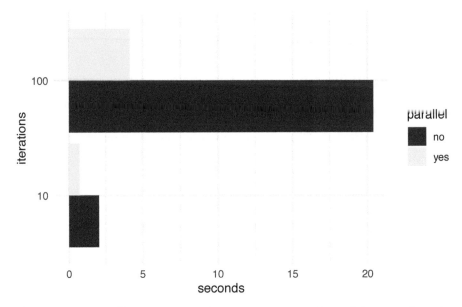

Figure 11.11: Comparison of computation time (shorter bar is faster).

11.10 Good Practice

Even though I cannot really aim for a comprehensive section on the *Do's and Dont's*, I would like to share a few common-sense practices here. If you are interested in a more thorough but rather R specific collection, take a look at the wonderful online book *What They Forgot to Tell Us About R*: https://rstats.wtf/.

Do NOT Set Static Working Directories in Your Code

Like `C:\Users\MatthiasBannert\My Documents\R Course\`. Locations that only exist in your own environment have you set up for trouble before you even started.

Please,

- resist that visceral urge to define the project root folder somewhere at the beginning of your code because your collaborators usually do not have a directory on their machine that bears your name. That might not even use the same operating system. And before you ask, simply putting the neutrally named folder on a shared NAS storage or service such as Dropbox is not really better.

- avoid spaces in folder and file names. Though modern operating systems and most languages can handle spaces, you might need to escape certain characters and make a beginner's life much harder. The same holds for umlauts and other hieroglyphic characters. Simply use lower-case and either kebab-case or snake_case.

- work with projects of your favorite IDE. The idea of projects is to make a folder the document root of your project. That way, your code can reference to other files inside this project root in relative fashion, no matter where the project itself is located.

Take Time To Learn How To Play the "Piano"

There is no need to become a *vim* virtuoso (that's essentially Lang Lang status on a computer keyboard), but make sure to learn some basic shortcuts of your environment that help you avoid touching the mouse or trackpad. Like `ctrl+L` to clear the screen, `cmd+tab` to switch between applications, `cmd+w` to close windows, `ctrl+number` to switch between tabs and, most importantly, some shortcut to execute the selected line of code (often `cmd+enter`, `ctrl+enter` or `shift+enter` depending on your operating system). Note that this is really not so much about a specific programming language, but more about the environment you work in.

Manage Dependencies at the Project Level

JavaScript projects manage dependencies in their lock files, Python projects have their requirements.txt files, and R has the {renv} package (Ushey and Wickham 2023). All these scripting languages *can* keep track of the exact library versions used in a project.

```
pip freeze |
  grep -v "pkg-resources" > requirements.txt
```

The above pip command extracts dependencies from a Python project's folder and writes it to a requirements file. Nevertheless, because there is no build process, scripting languages do not enforce keeping track of library versions necessarily. And even though it is common sense in engineering, it took data science, R in particular, quite a while to really establish going the extra mile and keep track of a project's dependencies. For many, an R *project A* simply loads a few libraries, does its job, while another *R project B* loads its libraries and does another job – all on the same local machine. After a few more projects, we decided to upgrade R to the next minor release, e.g., go from 4.1. to 4.2. which cause reinstalling all the extensions packages. It is a very safe bet that at least one of the packages we use gets its own update (or two) between two R minor releases. When all projects share the same library, your project that has just started after the latest package release may benefit from the latest feature of a package, while another project might break because its code is affected by a breaking change. Given that most packages are not large in size, I encourage everyone starting a programming with data project to embrace project-based library version management early on.

Glossary

Term	Description
API	Application Programming Interface
CamelCase	Convention to spell file, variable or function names reminiscent of a camel, e.g., doSomething().
CMS	Content Management System.
Console	Also known as terminal, the console is an interface which takes written user commands. Bash is one of the most popular terminals on OS level, but scripting languages like Python and R have consoles to communicate with their interpreter,too.
Deployment	The art of delivering a piece of software to production.
Endpoint	Part of an API, a generic URL that follows a logic that can be exploited to automate machine-to-machine data exchange.
Fork	A clone of a repository that you (usually) do not own.
GUI	Graphical User Interface.
IDE	Integrated Development Environment.
Kebab Case	Spelling convention less known than snake case and camel case, kebap case looks like this: my-super-folder.

(continued)

Term	Description
Lexical Scoping	Look-up of variables in parent environments when they can't be found in the current environment. Be aware that this is the default behavior of R.
Merge Request	See Pull Request.
OS	Operating System.
OSS	Open Source Software.
Pull Request (PR)	Request to join a feature branch into another branch, e.g., main branch. Sometimes it's also called merge request.
Regular Expression	Pattern to extract specific parts from a text, find stuff in a text.
REPL	read-eval-print-loop.
Reproducible Example	A self-contained code example, including the data it needs to run.
Reverse Dependency	Inverted dependency, another library or piece of code that depends on the code at hand.
Snake_case	Convention to spell file, variable or function names reminiscant of a snake, e.g., do_something().
Stack	selection of software used in a project.
SQL	Structured Query Language.
Swimlanes	(Online) Board of columns (lanes). Lanes progress from from left to right and carry issues.
Throughput Problem	A bottleneck which can be mitigated by parallelization, e.g., multiple containers running in parallel.

(continued)

Term	Description
Transactional database	database optimized for production systems. Such a database is good at reading and writing individual rows without affecting the other and while taking care of data integrity.
Virtual Machine (VM)	A virtual computer hosted on your computer. Often used to run another OS inside your main OS for testing purposes.

References

Allaire, J. J., Charles Teague, Carlos Scheidegger, Yihui Xie, and Christophe Dervieux. 2022. *Quarto* (version 1.2). https://doi.org/10.5281/zenodo.5960048.

Allaire, JJ, Yihui Xie, Jonathan McPherson, Javier Luraschi, Kevin Ushey, Aron Atkins, Hadley Wickham, Joe Cheng, Winston Chang, and Richard Iannone. 2022. *Rmarkdown: Dynamic Documents for r.* https://github.com/rstudio/rmarkdown.

Bannert, Matthias, and Severin Thoeni. 2022. *Kofdata: Get Data from the 'KOF Datenservice' API.* https://CRAN.R-project.org/package=kofdata.

Bannert, Matthias, Severin Thoeni, and Stéphane Bisinger. 2023. *Tstools: A Time Series Toolbox for Official Statistics.* https://CRAN.R-project.org/package=tstools.

Beg, Marijan, Juliette Taka, Thomas Kluyver, Olexandr Konovalov, Min Ragan-Kelly, Nicolas M. Thiéry, and Hans Fangohr. 2021. "Using Jupyter for Reproducible Scientific Workflows." *CoRR* abs/2102.09562. https://arxiv.org/abs/2102.09562.

Bengtsson, Henrik. 2021. "A Unifying Framework for Parallel and Distributed Processing in r Using Futures." *The R Journal* 13 (2): 208–27. https://doi.org/10.32614/RJ-2021-048.

Bezanson, Jeff, Alan Edelman, Stefan Karpinski, and Viral B Shah. 2017. "Julia: A Fresh Approach to Numerical Computing." *SIAM Review* 59 (1): 65–98. https://doi.org/10.1137/141000671.

Bostock, Michael, Vadim Ogievetsky, and Jeffrey Heer. 2011. "D3 Data-Driven Documents." *IEEE Transactions on Visualization and Computer Graphics* 17 (12): 2301–9. https://doi.org/10.1109/TVCG.2011.185.

Chang, Winston. 2021. *R6: Encapsulated Classes with Reference Semantics.* https://CRAN.R-project.org/package=R6.

Chang, Winston, and Barbara Borges Ribeiro. 2021. *Shinydashboard: Create Dashboards with 'Shiny'*. https://CRAN.R-project.org/package=shinydashboard.

Chang, Winston, Joe Cheng, JJ Allaire, Carson Sievert, Barret Schloerke, Yihui Xie, Jeff Allen, Jonathan McPherson, Alan Dipert, and Barbara Borges. 2022. *Shiny: Web Application Framework for r*. https://CRAN.R-project.org/package=shiny.

Dervieux, Christophe, JJ Allaire, Rich Iannone, Alison Presmanes Hill, and Yihui Xie. 2022. *Distill: 'R Markdown' Format for Scientific and Technical Writing*. https://CRAN.R-project.org/package=distill.

Fay, C., S. Rochette, V. Guyader, and C. Girard. 2021. *Engineering Production-Grade Shiny Apps*. Chapman & Hall/CRC the r Series. CRC Press. https://books.google.ch/books?id=qExDEAAAQBAJ.

Hernangómez, Diego. 2021. "Cffr: Generate Citation File Format Metadata for r Packages." *Journal of Open Source Software* 6 (67): 3900. https://doi.org/10.21105/joss.03900.

Hunter, J. D. 2007. "Matplotlib: A 2D Graphics Environment." *Computing In Science & Engineering* 9 (3): 90–95.

Joo, Rocío et al. 2022. "Ten Simple Rules to Host an Inclusive Conference." *PLOS Computational Biology* 18 (7): 1–13. https://doi.org/10.1371/journal.pcbi.1010164.

Landau, William Michael. 2021. "The Targets r Package: A Dynamic Make-Like Function-Oriented Pipeline Toolkit for Reproducibility and High-Performance Computing." *Journal of Open Source Software* 6 (57): 2959. https://doi.org/10.21105/joss.02959.

Li, Deqing, Honghui Mei, Yi Shen, Shuang Su, Wenli Zhang, Junting Wang, Ming Zu, and Wei Chen. 2018. "ECharts: A Declarative Framework for Rapid Construction of Web-Based Visualization." *Visual Informatics* 2 (2): 136–46. https://doi.org/https://doi.org/10.1016/j.visinf.2018.04.011.

Mersmann, Olaf. 2021. *Microbenchmark: Accurate Timing Functions*. https://CRAN.R-project.org/package=microbenchmark.

Pedersen, Thomas Lin, and David Robinson. 2022. *Gganimate: A Grammar of Animated Graphics.* https://CRAN.R-project.org/package=gganimate.

Perepolkin, Dmytro. 2023. *Polite: Be Nice on the Web.* https://CRAN.R-project.org/package=polite.

Richardson, Neal, Ian Cook, Nic Crane, Dewey Dunnington, Romain François, Jonathan Keane, Dragoș Moldovan-Grünfeld, Jeroen Ooms, and Apache Arrow. 2022. *Arrow: Integration to 'Apache' 'Arrow'.* https://CRAN.R-project.org/package=arrow.

Sax, Christoph, and Dirk Eddelbuettel. 2018. "Seasonal Adjustment by X-13ARIMA-SEATS in R." *Journal of Statistical Software* 87 (11): 1–17. https://doi.org/10.18637/jss.v087.i11.

Schloerke, Barret, and Jeff Allen. 2022. *Plumber: An API Generator for r.* https://CRAN.R-project.org/package=plumber.

Sink, Eric. 2011. *Version Control by Example.* 1st ed. PYOW Sports Marketing.

Ushey, Kevin, and Hadley Wickham. 2023. *Renv: Project Environments.* https://CRAN.R-project.org/package=renv.

van der Loo, MPJ. 2020. "A Method for Deriving Information from Running r Code." *The R Journal,* Accepted for publication. https://arxiv.org/abs/2002.07472.

Vilhuber, Lars, Marie Connolly, Miklós Koren, Joan Llull, and Peter Morrow. 2022. *A template README for social science replication packages.* https://doi.org/10.5281/zenodo.7293838.

Wickham, H. 2015. *R Packages: Organize, Test, Document, and Share Your Code.* O'Reilly Media. https://r-pkgs.org/.

Wickham, Hadley. 2011. "Testthat: Get Started with Testing." *The R Journal* 3: 5–10. https://journal.r-project.org/archive/2011-1/RJournal_2011-1_Wickham.pdf.

———. 2016. *Ggplot2: Elegant Graphics for Data Analysis.* Springer-Verlag New York. https://ggplot2.tidyverse.org.

———. 2019. *Advanced r.* 2nd ed. Chapman & Hall/CRC the r Series. Taylor & Francis.

———. 2021. *Mastering Shiny.* O'Reilly Media, Incorporated. https://books.google.ch/books?id=ha1CzgEACAAJ.

———. 2022a. *Rvest: Easily Harvest (Scrape) Web Pages.* https://CRAN.R-project.org/package=rvest.

———. 2022b. *Stringr: Simple, Consistent Wrappers for Common String Operations.* https://CRAN.R-project.org/package=stringr.

Wickham, Hadley, Jennifer Bryan, Malcolm Barrett, and Andy Teucher. 2023. *Usethis: Automate Package and Project Setup.* https://CRAN.R-project.org/package=usethis.

Wickham, Hadley, Peter Danenberg, Gábor Csárdi, and Manuel Eugster. 2022. *Roxygen2: In-Line Documentation for r.* https://CRAN.R-project.org/package=roxygen2.

Wickham, Hadley, and Garrett Grolemund. 2017. *R for Data Science: Import, Tidy, Transform, Visualize, and Model Data.* 1st ed. O'Reilly Media, Inc.

Wickham, Hadley, Jay Hesselberth, and Maëlle Salmon. 2022. *Pkgdown: Make Static HTML Documentation for a Package.* https://CRAN.R-project.org/package=pkgdown.

Xie, Yihui, Alison Presmanes Hill, and Amber Thomas. 2017. *Blogdown: Creating Websites with R Markdown.* Boca Raton, Florida: Chapman; Hall/CRC. https://bookdown.org/yihui/blogdown/.

Zheng, Chunmei, Guomei He, and Zuojie Peng. 2015. "A Study of Web Information Extraction Technology Based on Beautiful Soup." *J. Comput.* 10: 381–87.

Index

Milton Keynes UK
Ingram Content Group UK Ltd.
UKHW051535141024
449569UK00001B/50

9 781032 261645